FRANKLIN COUNTY GEORGIA

Superior Court Minutes

- 1814-1818

(Volume #1)

Compiled by:
Michael A. Ports

Southern Historical Press
Greenville, South Carolina

Copyright 2018
By: Michael A. Ports

All rights reserved. No part of this publication may be reproduced, stored in a retrieval system, transmitted in any form, posted on to the web in any form or by any means without the prior written permission of the publisher.

Please direct all correspondence and orders to:

www.southernhistoricalpress.com
or
**SOUTHERN HISTORICAL PRESS, Inc.
PO BOX 1267
375 West Broad Street
Greenville, SC   29601**
southernhistoricalpress@gmail.com

ISBN #0-89308-929-X

Printed in the United States of America

Introduction

On February 25, 1784, the Georgia General Assembly created Franklin County from lands ceded by the Cherokee and Creek the previous year, and designated Carnesville as the seat of its government. Portions of Franklin County were taken to form Madison County in 1811, Hart County in 1853, Banks County in 1858, and Stephens County in 1905. The judges of the Superior Courts, elected to serve three-year terms, held court in each county at least twice per year, as they traveled from county to county within their circuit. The Superior Court held jurisdiction over all criminal matters, most civil cases, especially those involving title to land, appeals from Inferior Court and Justices Court decisions, divorces, admissions to the bar, grand juries, and registration of land

deeds.

The following transcription comes from the microfilm photographed in 1964 at the courthouse in Carnesville, Georgia, by the Genealogical Society of Salt Lake City, Utah, and available at the Georgia Archives in Morrow, Georgia. The heading on the microfilm reads

**Franklin
County
Georgia
Superior Court**

and

**Superior Court
Minutes**

Index

1814 - 1818

While the heading apparently indicates that the court minutes are indexed, the original record volume contains no index. However, a complete full-name index follows the transcription. The reader should know that a lone surname in the index indicates that no first name appears in the minutes, for example Mr. Smith or Smith & Company. An index entry such as Smith, ___ indicates that a first name was entered into the minutes, but has been obscured by an ink blot, smear, tear, or other imperfection. The clerk did not number the pages, instead usually, but not always, entering the court term at the top of each page, for example, *April Term 1817*. To assist the researcher in locating the original pages, the symbol ___ is placed at the bottom left-hand corner of each original page. By noting the date, or at least the court term, of an individual entry in the minutes, the researcher should not have too much difficulty in locating that entry in the original record or on the microfilm copy.

In the upper right-hand corner of the inside cover, the clerk wrote *100 3 Henry*, the significance of which is unknown. In the lower left-hand corner, the clerk wrote the letter *W* and underneath it the word *Washington*, the significance of which also is unknown. In the center near the top of the inside cover, the Clerk wrote

Franklin County
Courts – Superior – Minutes
Apr. 1814 – Oct. 1818

The minutes begin on April 11, 1814, at the start of the April Term, and continue in chronological order through the end of the October Term 1818. Following the formal adjournment of the last term, the minutes include the record of one defendant entering an appeal on two cases and another defendant entering a stay of execution, both just days after that adjournment.

Maxfield H. Payne served as clerk during the entire period covered by the minutes and almost invariably signed the minutes at the start and end of each day's proceedings. Based upon the different handwriting, as many as three or possibly more deputy clerks entered some of the proceedings, but their names are not recorded. Young Gresham presided as judge from the April Term 1814 through the October Term 1816. John M. Dooly presided as judge starting with the April Term 1817 through the end of the minutes. The original signatures of the three men appear numerous times throughout the minutes. The minutes contain numerous other original signatures, mostly of attorneys filing various motions, petitions, and affidavits as well as those parties filing bonds for appeals and stays of execution, as well as their securities.

For the most part, the handwriting is legible, and the quality of the microfilm is good, making the reading and transcription process straightforward and not too difficult, although the handwriting of one particular clerk is not much better than a scrawl. The occasional ink blot, smear, or other imperfection is noted within brackets, for example [blot] or [faint]. The transcription follows Sperry's recommended guidelines for reading early American handwriting.[1] Generally, the transcription maintains the overall format of the minutes, but presents the case citations, jury panels, lists of witnesses, signatures, and other court proceedings in a standard and consistent format. No grammar or spelling errors are corrected in the transcription, although a few commas, semicolons, apostrophes, and periods are added for clarity. The clerks entered a vertical squiggly line to delineate case citations, affidavit and petition headings, and signature citations, replicated by the symbol } in the transcription. Following each original signature, the clerk entered a symbol consisting of the capital letters "L" and "S" encircled by a squiggly line, evidently indicting the individual's seal, as follows

That symbol is not included in the transcription.

Sometimes the clerk formed the letters "a" and "o" in a very similar manner, making abbreviations like Jas. and Jos. and surnames Bagg and Bogg or Shannan and Shannon difficult to distinguish. At other times, the letters "a" and "u" are too similar to

---

[1] Sperry, Kip, *Reading Early American Handwriting*. Genealogical Publishing Company, Baltimore, Maryland, Sixth Printing, 2008.

differentiate such names as Burton and Barton or Barnett and Burnett, or Barns and Burns. In a similar manner, the names Edmond and Edmund can be difficult to distinguish. The formation of the letters "n" and "r" at the end of surnames sometimes appear to be the same. Inavariably, the formation of the capital letters "I" and "J" are identical. Determining which letter usually not difficult when the first letter of a name, but almost entirely a guess when a lone middle initial. The clerk often crossed the letter "t" by extending the horizontal line across the entire word, making it difficult to distinguish between such surnames as Walters and Watters. Compounding the problem, he sometimes neglected to cross any "t" in a word, making a "t" appear to be an "l." Careful researchers will consult the original record or the microfilm copy to either confirm the transcription or formulate an alternative interpretation of the clerk's handwriting.

The book is dedicated to the memory of the author's fifth great grandparents William and Margaret (Harbin) Suttle, their son Macajah and his wife Sarah Ford, their daughter Margaret and her husband Joseph Willis, and their daughter Nancy and her husband John M. Smith, all residents of Franklin County during this period. Many thanks are offered the kind, patient, and generous staff of the Georgia Archives for their assistance and suggestions, not only in locating the original records, but in understanding their historical context. Thanks also are offered LaBruce Lucas of the Southern Historical Press for his sage professional advice and counsel. Special thanks are offered to Marcia Tremonti for her patience and encouragement throughout the entire process of transcription and publication.

Superior Court Minutes

April Term 1814

The Superior Court of Franklin County met on the Eleventh day, being the Second Monday, in April 1814.

Present, His Honor Judge Gresham.

According to the Exegence of a Writ of Venire to him directed, the high Sheriff of Said County returned Said Writ into Court, with the following persons Summoned & Sworn as Grand Jurors, Viz.

1. John R. Brown
2. Robert Malone
3. Asa Allen
4. Saml H. Everett
5. James Hooper
6. George Stovall
7. Elias Baker
8. Capt Benjn Cleveland
9. John Neal
10. Littleton Meeks
11. Edmund King, Ju^r
12. Edmund Henley
13. Robert Walters
14. Thompson Epperson
15. Richard Hooper
16. William Ash, Se^r
17. Stephen Poe
18. John Bush
19. Joshua Hudson
20. Henry Smith
21. Samuel Shannon
22. William Hackett
23. John Hooper

Petit Jurors N° 1

1. Thos Lenoir
2. Groves Yarbrough
3. John Bellamy
4. David Miller
5. Benjn Hifield
6. Henry Barrons
7. Robert Saxon
8. George Carrell
9. James Hargrove
10. Starling Strange
11. Ephraim Mabry
12. Moses Sanders, Ju^r

April Term 1814

The State   } vs
} Ind^t Assault
David Allison }

In this Case, Came the Security, James Hollingsworth, into Court & delivered up the defendant & was thereupon discharged.
Petit Jury N° 2

1. Benjn Baker, Se^r
2. Manoah Saxon
3. Thos Nunn
4. Josiah Stovall
5. Thos White
6. Aris Cox
7. Saml Tait
8. John Ayers
9. George C. Taylor
10. James Williamson
11. Richard Malden
12. Washington Allen

John McDaid, Abel Peak, Thos Sparks, Senr, Gabriel Smith, Phillip Pruitt, James Wilkison, Asa Leach, James Ramsey, Reuben Payne, John Anthony, Sampson Bobo

Being summoned to serve as Petit Jurors at the present Term & neglected so to do, it is ordered that they pay each the sum of fifteen Dollars, unless they file in the Clerk's Office of this Court Satisfactory excuse under oath within thirty Days after the opening of the present Term, & on their failure so to do the Clerk is ordered to issue separate executions against them for the amount of their Respective fines.

Nathl Statham }
    vs   } Trespass vi et arms
Charles Payne }

Jury N° 1

We, the Jurors, find for the plaintiff twenty five dollars, with Cost of Suit.

                                        Ja^s Hargroves, foreman

---

April Term 1814

The State   }   vs
} Ind^t Assault
Joshua Hooper }

True Bill.   John R. Brown, Forman

The State   }   vs
} Ind^t Assault
Joshua Hooper }

True Bill.   John R. Brown, foreman

The State   }   vs
} Ind^t Assault
David Ellison }

True Bill.   John R. Brown, foreman

The State   }   vs
} Ind^t Assault
Winkfield Bagwell }

True Bill.   John R. Brown, foreman

The State   }   vs
} Ind.^t Assault
Cleverly Phillips }
True Bill.   John R. Brown, foreman

John Doe, Ex dem   }
Charles Quigly   }
    vs   } Ejectment
Richard Roe, in   }
Possession,   } Jesse
David & others }

Non Suit

The Admrs of Amos }
Brather, dec^d   }
    vs   } Trover Franklin Superior Court
John Westbrooks   } Verdict for Plffs Special Jury

To the plaintiffs, or their attorney, please take notice that I Shall, on the first day of the Next Term, or so soon thereafter as consel can be heard, move the Honorable Court for a new trial in the above Case on the following Grounds, to wit

---

April Term 1814

1st Because the Special Jury found Contrary to evidence & the principles of Justice & Equity.

2nd Because the Court overruled a release offered by the defendant from One of the plaintiffs, which ought to have been admitted.

                              Harris, Cook, & Dooly, for Deft

It is agreed by Consel that the two above Grounds, say the first & last Grounds, for a new trial be argued next week at Elbert, & if on hearing argument, the Court Shall Grant Rule Ni Si, it Shall be considered as entered on the Minutes of Franklin Court.

14th April   Geo Cook, Df atty
                                  Thos P. Carnes, plffs' atty

Elbert Superior Court } April
Term 1813   }

The above Case, having been now been argued, The Court ordered, that the Rule Ni Si be Granted & this order, together with the above Grounds for said rule & the Consent of Counsel, be entered on the minutes of Franklin Superior Court.

Young Gresham, Judge   Superior Court

The State } vs } Ind.^t Grand Larceny
Charity Woodall }

No Bill.   John R. Brown, Foreman

April Term 1814

John Doe, Ex dem   }
the heirs of   }
Thomas Bray, deceased   }
    vs   } Ejectment
Richd Roe, cas^l Ejector }
& Jacob Whisenhunt,   }
Tenant in possession   }

Dismissed.

The Court then Adjourned untill to morrow morning Eight O'Clock.

Test. Maxfield H. Payne, C. S. C.

Ex^d   Young Gresham

The Court then met according to adjournment on tuesday the 12th of April 1814.

Present, his honor Judge Gresham.

The fine of John McDow for nonattendance on yesterday is remitted.

Charity Woodall, Spinster }
    vs   } Slander
Alexander Williamson   }

Jury N° 1

We, the Jurors, find for the plaintiff four hundred dollars, with Cost of Suit.

                           Ja^s Hargroves, Foreman

Joseph Woodall, who was bail for Israel Blagg, delivered up the defendant Blagg, who was thereupon discharged.

April Term 1814

Robert Cimmins, Appellant }
    vs   } Trover

Isaac Strickland, Respondant }

Jury Sworn.

Nonsuit.
  1. Elias Baker   7. Richard Hooper
  2. John Neal   8. William Ash, Senr
  3. Littleton Meeks   9. Stephen Poe
  4. Edmund King, J^r 10. Joshua Hudson
  5. Edmund Henley   11. William Hackett
  6. Robert Watters   12. John Hooper

The Court then Adjourned untill to morrow morning Eight O'Clock.

Test. Maxfield H. Payne, Clk

Ex^d Young Gresham

The Court met On Wednesday morning according to Adjournment April 13th 1814.

Present, his honor Judge Gresham.

James Wilkinson produced an affidavit that he was not summoned as a Juror, & thereupon the fine was remitted.

April Term 1814

Robert Cimmins, appellant }
   vs   } Trover
Isaac Strickland, Respondant }

Nonsuit.

On motion of Counsel for Respondent, It is ordered that the appellant Shew Cause on the first day of the next term, or so Soon thereafter as Counsel can be heard, why the Nonsuit in this Case Should not be Set aside, the Case reinstituted, and proceed to trial before a Special Jury.

Jury N° 1, except James Williamson in place of Benjamin Hifield.
The State   }
  vs   } Ind^t Adultery & Fornication
Benjamin Stoydon }
& Sarah Hall   }

Nol proseque.

The State }
  vs   } Ind^t Invegeling a negro
Joseph Bevan   }

Nol proseque.

Jury Nº 1

1. Thos Lenoir	7. Robert Saxon
2. Groves Yarborough	8. George Cairrell
3. John Bellamy	9. James Hargroves
4. David Miller	10. Sterling Strange
5. James Williamson	11. Ephraim Mabry
6. Henry Barrons	12. Moses Sanders, Junr

April Term 1814

The State }
    vs   } Indt Petit Larceny
John Everett & }
Israel Blagg }

True Bill.   John R. Brown, Forman

The State }
    vs   } Indt horse Stealing
John Everett & }
Israel Blagg }

True Bill.   John R. Brown, Foreman

The State }
    vs   } Indt Assault
William Martin }

True Bill.   John R. Brown, foreman

The State   }   vs
} Indt assault
Andrew Hamilton }

True Bill.   John R. Brown, Foreman

The State } vs } Indt Petit Larceny
Larking Purdue }

No Bill.   John R. Brown, Forman

The State   }   vs
} Indt Inveigling
Joseph Bevan }

On motion of Counsel, Stating to the Court that Joseph Bevan & David McCormick are bound in a recognizance Conditioned for the appearance of said Bevan at this Court, and a Noli Proseque having been entered by Consent. It is ordered, that said recognizance be discharged and go without day.

April Term 1814

The State }
vs } Ind^t Petit Larceny Wm Hooper }

Jury N° 1

1. Thos Lenoir
2. Grove Yarborough
3. John Bellamy
4. David Miller
5. James Williamson
6. Henry Barrons
7. Robert Saxon
8. George Carrell
9. James Hargroves
10. Sterling Strange
11. Epham Mabry
12. Moses Sanders, Junr

We, the Jury, find the Defendant William Hooper not Guilty, that the prosecution is malicious, & the prosecutor pay the Cost.

Ja^s Hargrove, Forman

Isaac Strickland, applt }
    vs } Ejectment
Wilson Strickland, Resp^t }

Settled at Respt's Cost.

Isaac Strickland, appellant }
    vs } Case
Wilson Strickland, Respondant }

Settled at Respt's Cost.

Isaac Strickland, appellant }
    vs } Case
Wilson Strickland, Respondant }

Settled at Respt's Cost.

Wilson Strickland }
    vs } Bill in Equity
Isaac Strickland }

Settled at Wilson Strickland's Cost.

April Term 1814

Wilson Strickland }
vs } Bill in Equity & Injunction Isaac Strickland }

Settled at Wilson Strickland's Cost.

The State }
vs } Ind^t Assault & False imprisonment
John West }
Swan Harden & } Salathiah
Bradberry }

Jury N° 1

We, the Jurors, find the Prisoners guilty.

         Ja^s Hargrove, Forman

The Court then Adjourned untill to morrow morning Eight O'Clock.

Test. Maxfield H. Payne, Clk

Ex^d Young Gresham

The Court met on Thursday morning according to Adjournment, being the 14th day of April 1814.

Present, his honor Judge Gresham.

The State } vs } Ind^t Horse Stealing
John Vaughan }
& Mathew Cox }
No Bill.   John R. Brown, Foreman

April Term 1814

The Solicitor General having been unexpectedly caled from this Court by the Sickness of his family.

It is ordered, that Duncan G. Campbell, Esqr be & he is hereby appointed Sol Genl pro Tem & his acts as such for the balance of this Term are to be held & considered as legal & valid.

Edmund King } vs
} Bill in Equity
Samuel Phillips }
Edmund Henley }

William Henley }
Jane Henley & }
Mary Henley }

In this Case, the Complainant having obtained Leave to amend his bill & the amended bill having been Served & not answered, it is ordered, that the Respondents Served in the amended bill answer in thirty days or the bill be taken pro Confesso.

James Hargroves } and wife
} vs } Bill in Equity
Samuel McKie }
William McKie }

On motion of Counsel for the Complainant. It is ordered, that the defendants Shew cause on the first day of the Next term, or soon thereafter as Counsel can be heard, why the appeal Should not be entered nun protune and in Case the appeal is ordered by the Court be entered, that the Case Stand for trial at October term next.

James Oliver, Respd[t] }
   vs } Case
Isaac J. Barratt } et al
Exors applt[s] }

We, the Special Jury, find for the Respondant the Sum of one hundred & fifty dollars & thirty nine Cents, with interest on the note, & cost of suit.

Asa Allen, foreman

April Term 1814

The State } vs
} Ind[t] assault
Andrew Hamilton }

Fined thirty dollars.

Hugh Nesbit }
   vs } Debt
John D. Terrel & }
Ge[o] Drury Paine }

We Confess judgment to the plaintiff for the Sum of four hundred and ninety one dollars fifty six and one quarter Cents, with interest and Costs.

John D. Terrell, for the late firm of
Terrell & Paine

The State }
    vs } Ind^t Assl^t & false imprisonment
John West }
Swan Harden & }

Salathiah Bradbury }

The parties appeared to receive Sentence, when the following fines were imposed. Swan Hardin fined eight dollars & John West & Salathiel Bradberry find in the Sum of five dollars each.

Elisha Wilkinson, appellant }
    vs } Case
Benjamin Dorsey, Respondant } Jury
Sworn.

    1. John R. Brown   7. John Hooper
    2. Robert Malone   8. Saml Shannon
    3. Edmund King, Junr   9. Joshua Hudson
    4. Edmund Henley   10. Benjⁿ Cleveland
    5. Thompson Epperson   11. Robert Walters
    6. William Hackett   12. James Hooper

We, the Jury, find for the Respondent three hundred & two dollars & forty Cents, with Interest & Cost, & three pr Cent on the principal sum due for a frivolous appeal.

                                                John R. Brown, forman

---

April Term 1814

John D. Terrell & }
George D. Paine, appt^s }
    vs } Case
John Swift, Resp^t }

Jury as in the Case before.

We, the Jury, find for the Respondent the Sum of two hundred dollars, with Interest & Cost of Suit.

                                                John R. Brown, forman

Sampson Bobo who was find by the Court in Sum of fifteen dollars has produced & affidavit & there upon was discharged from the fine.

On motion of Walton Harris for himself & others, Stating that on the fifteenth day of April 1812, a bond was Entered into by him, Edward Adams, Hugh Montgomery, & others for the Purpose of Securing a negro man Daniel then delivered to Bartimus Runnels from being Removed out of the County of Jackson untill Edmund Henley Could prosecute a Suit at Law in Jackson County for Said negroe against said Bartimus, and the Said Edmund having failed so to do from the time aforesaid untill this day. It is ordered, that the Said Edmund Shew Cause on or before the first day of the Next Term why said bond Should not be annuled & Set aside, otherwise it will be annulled & Set aside.

George Mathews }
    vs   } Case
James McDonald }

Jury Nº 2

We find for the Plaintiff thirty dollars Eighty Cents, with Interest & Cost.

                                    Josiah Stovall, Foreman

April Term 1814

Freadrick Beall, appellant   }
    vs   } Debt
William & Christopher M. Slocum, } for
the use of Hugh Taylor, Resp[ts] }

Special Jury as before.

We, the Special Jury, find for the Respondant the Sum of Eight hundred & Sixty three dollars and twenty six Cents, with interest & Cost of Suit.

                                    John R. Brown, Forman

Jordan Lacy } vs } Trespass vi et armis
William A. Blackburn }

Settled at Defendant's Cost.

Joseph Yates } vs } Assault & Battery
Christopher Baker }
& Green Baker   }

Settled at defendant's Cost.

Georgia   }
Franklin County } Presentments of the Grand Jury of the County aforesaid at April Term 1814

The war in which America is now engaged with Great Britain and her dependences was predicated on injuries which could not otherwise be redressed. Where Government called it Citizens to its standard in defence of those rights dear to man. Franklin by her Volunteers unanimous were amongst the first to Step forward. The privations and

April Term 1814

perrils inseperable from a [blur] life to thence ever in fate embarrassed. Their Country Called. Its mandate from principal was imperative. They marched. Their lives or Death as providence denoted. The Battles of their Country they fought, if they to the bosoms of their families have enturned it, is the gift of heaven. This Jury fully appreciate the worth and patriotism of their brave countrymen, a recollection of whose Services perlingly exceeded by the battle of Autosa & the midnight attack of the Savage foe. The survivors of those memorable events are entitled to our warmest thanks & the memories of those who found honourable graves shall be religiously cherished. May their great examples be emulated by the present generation & may positively be boastful of their deathless horrors. We return our hearty acknowledgements to his honor Judge Gresham for his patient & assiduous attention to the business of long & laborious Term. We recommend that these our presentments be published in the Athens Gazette.

            John R. Brown

April Term 1814

Edmund King, Ju^r	Richard Hooper
Thompson Epperson	Benjamin Cleveland
James Hooper	Littleton Meeks
Henry Smith	George Stovall
Saml H. Everett	Asa Allen
Saml Shannon	Robert Waters
Wm Ash, Senr	John Hudson
Edmond Henly	Robert Malonee
Stephen Poe	John Bask
	Elias Baker
	Wm Hackett
	John Hooper

The Presentments of the grand Jury being taken of. It is ordered that they be published pursuant to the request therein contained.

The Court then Adjourned untill to morrow Nine O'Clock.

Test. Maxfield H. Payne, Clk
Ex^d Young Gresham

April Term 1814

Grand Jurors for October Term 1814

 1. John Womack   19. Wm Holley

2. Fred{^{k}} Beall
3. James Blair
4. Rich{^{d}} Wood
5. Adam Whisenhunt
6. Charles Rice
7. Rich{^{d}} Allan
8. Darby Henley
9. Isaac J. Barrett
10. John Jenkins
11. Redf{^{ern}} Weems
12. Joseph Watters
13. Winsette Foreman
14. Aaron Campbell
15. Tho{^{s}} Hollingsworth
16. Stephen Harrington
17. Tho{^{s}} Payn, S{^{r}}
18. Rob{^{t}} Banneville

20. Charles England
21. Swan Hardin
22. John Mayfield
23. W{^{m}} Jones Capt{^{n}}
24. Sam{^{l}} Hearden
25. Robert Hackett
26. John Garrisson
27. James Allan
28. Edmund King, Sen{^{r}}
29. W{^{m}} Pulliam
30. James Riley
31. Abner Dunnigan
32. Reuben Shotwell
33. Green H. Little
34. Benj{^{n}} Dorsey
35. John Sanders, S{^{r}}
36. Moses Sanders

Petit Jurors drawn for October Term 1814

1. Joel Laurens
2. Jesse Putman
3. John Gober
4. [smear] Y. Harrison
5. Jack Gober
6. John Clarkson

7. Absalom Parnell
8. Tho{^{s}} Savage
9. Tho{^{s}} Clark, Jun{^{r}}
10. Rich{^{d}} Halcomb
11. Joel Hunt
12. Tho{^{s}} Ivey

13. Archibald Cockburn
14. William Wilson
15. Edward Maynard
16. Peter Brown
17. Rich{^{d}} Bond, Jun{^{r}}
18. Timothy Terrall
19. George [smear] Taylor
20. Hutchins Barton
21. Thomas Gober
22. James Cail
23. Richard Gray
24. James Mercer
25. John Temples
26. Jacob Redwine
27. Atkins Tabor
28. Enoch Brady
29. W{^{m}} Eddins
30. Robert Langfared, J{^{r}}

31. Richard Hooper
32. Nathan{^{l}} Wofford
33. John M. Gray
34. Benj{^{a}} Whitehead
35. John Dorsey
36. Joseph White
37. Patrick Mabry
38. Deveroux Jarrott
39. Sam{^{l}} Morgan
40. Robert Walters, Jun{^{r}}
41. Louis Williams
42. Joseph Dobbins
43. Thomas Blair
44. Elijah Hall
45. Rob{^{t}} Bonds
46. Charles Sissons
47. Isaac C. Seals
48. Isham McBee

Drawn in presence of & by Judge Gresham 15th April 1814.

Robert Hackett } Trespass
    vs   } on the Case
John D. Terrell }

Nonsuit.

Tyre Swift   }   vs
} Certiorari
Killis Walton, Esqr }

Sustained, proceedings below Set aside & a new trial before a Second Jury ordered.

April Term 1814

William Chisolm }
    vs   } Attachment
Charles Payne }

Jury N° 2

We, the Jury, find for the plaintiff the sum of two hundred and Seventy five dollars forty Nine & ¼ Cents, with Interest & Cost of Suit.

                                              Jo^s Stovall, F^m

Benjamin W. Rogers }
    vs   } Debt
Frederick Beall   }

I confess Judgment to the plaintiff for the Sum of Three Hundred and twenty two dollars forty six Cents, with Interest & Costs.

                                                Fred^k Beall

Joseph Bevan }
    vs   } Trover
John R. Brown }

Jury N° 2

We find for the plaintiff five hundred dollars, which may be discharged by delivery of George, now called Bob, in Ten days, with Cost of Suit.

                                                Jo^s Stovall, F^r

Dudley Jones   }
    vs   } Trespass vi et armis
Benjamin Dorsey }

Jury N° 2

We, the Jurors, find for the Defendant, with Cost.

Jo^s Stovall, F.

April Term 1814

Stephen Kitchen }
    vs   } Covenant
James Logan   }

Regula Generalis

It is ordered, that henceforth no applicant for admission to the practice of Law in this Circuit Shall be admitted untill proof Shall be exhibited to the Court of such applicants having arrived to the full age of Twenty One years. & that this Rule be Sent to the Clerks of the Several Courts in this circuit.

George   }

Madison County } Superior Court October Term 1813

I Certify that the foregoing is a true extract from the Minutes March 7th 1814.

James Long, Clk

Georgia } Franklin County
}

Joseph Bevan }
vs   }
John R. Brown }

Trover in Sup^r Court for negro George, alias Bob, & Verdict for plaff April Term 1814.

This is to Certify that the deft John R. Brown hath this day delivered to me, the atty for plff, Said negro George & he is received in full discharge of the foregoing Judgment, except the Costs.

15th April 1814   Duncan G. Campbell, Plffs Atty

The Court then Adjourned untill Court in Course.

15th April 1814

Ex^d Young Gresham

Test. Maxfield H. Payne, Clk S. C.

October Term 1814

The Superior Court of Franklin met on the tenth day of October, it being the Second monday in said month. Present, his honor Judge Gresham.

according to the exegince of a Writ of Venire to him directed, the high Sheriff of Said County returned Said Writ into Court, with the following persons Summoned & Sworn as Grand Jurors, Viz.

1. Frederick Beall
2. James Blair
3. John Garrisson
4. James Allan
5. William Jones
6. Thos Payne
7. John Mayfield
8. Samuel Headen
9. John Wormack
10. Robert Barnhill
11. William Holley
12. Joseph Watters
13. Adam Whisenhunt
14. Meredith Brown
15. Redfearn Wims
16. Abner Dunnigin
17. Darby Henley
18. Thos Hollingsworth
19. Sawan Harden
20. Moses Sanders
21. Benjn Dorsey
22. Reuben Shotwell
23. Charles Rice

October Term 1814

Petit Jury N° 1
1. Jesse Putman
2. Robert Harrison
3. John Clarkson
4. Joel Hunt
5. Archabald Cockburn
6. Jacob Redwine
7. Peter Brown
8. William Eddins
9. George Taylor
10. Richd Gray
11. James Mercer
12. John Temples

Nathan Smith }
    vs   } Case

William Spears }

Jury N° 1

We, the Jury, find for the plaintiff the Sum of twenty Seven dollars and forty two Cents, with interest & Cost of Suit.

$$\text{Ri}^\text{d}\text{ D. Gray, forman}$$

Wm Jacobs } vs } Case
Ambrose Blackburn }

We, the Jury, find for the plaintiff twenty Six dollars & fifty Cents, with interest & Cost.

$$\text{R}^\text{d}\text{ Gray, forman}$$

Doe, Ex dem } Simon
Terrell }
   vs } Ejectment
Roe, cas. Eject^r & }
William Tarsey } tenants
in possession }

Jury N° 1

We, the Jury, find for the plaintiff the premises in dispute, with Cost of Suit.

R. D. Gray, forman

October Term 1814

John Doe, ex dem }
Moses Herring }
   vs } Ejectment
Richard Roe, cas. Eject^r }
& Charles Warren }
tenant in possession }

Jury N° 1

We, the Jury, find for the plaintiff the premises in dispute, with Cost of Suit.

R. D. Gray, forman

The State   } vs
} Ind^t Assault
Isaac J. Barrett }

No Bill.   F. Beall, forman

Benjamin Dorsey }
    vs   } Trespass
Dudley Jones   }

Jury N° 1

We, the Jury, find for the plaintiff one hundred & fifty Dollars, with Costs of Suit.

                                            R. D. Gray, forman

The Court then adjourned untill to morrow morning Nine O'Clock.

Test. Maxfield H. Payne, Clk

Ex^d Young Gresham

The Court met According to adjournment on tuesday 11th October 1814.

present, his honor Judge Gresham.

October Term 1814

The Adm^{rs} of A. Bratcher, Dec^d, Appellants }
    vs   } Trover
Stephen Westbrooks, Respondant   }

Special Jury
       1. James Allan   7. Redfearn Wims
       2. Wm Jones   8. Abner Dunnigan
       3. Samuel Haden   9. Darby Henley
       4. John Wormack   10. Swan Harden
       5. Adam Whisenhunt   11. Reuben Shotwell
       6. Meredith Brown   12. Charles Rice

We, the Jury, find for the defendant, with cost of Suit.

                                          Ja^s Allan, Forman

The Court then adjourned untill tomorrow morning Eight O'Clock.

Test. Maxfield H. Payne, Clk

Ex^d Young Gresham

The Court then met according to adjournment on Wednesday, it being the 12th day of October 1814.

October Term 1814

Rob.t Commins, app.l }
    vs   } Nonsuit
Isaac Strickland   }

Rule on the part of Strickland that cummins shew cause why the nonsuit Should not be Set aside, and now at this term cause being Shewn, it ordered on motion that the Said Rule be discharged.

William Sansom }
    vs   } Trespass on the Case
George Sherill } Nonsuit.

Petit Jury N.o 1

    1. Jesse Putman   7. Tho.s Gober
    2. Robert Harrisson   8. W.m Eddins
    3. John Clarkson   9. George Taylor
    4. Joel Hunt   10. Richard Gray
    5. Archabald Cockburn   11. James Mercer
    6. Jacob Redwine   12. John Temples

The State   }
    vs   } Ind.t Horse Stealing
John Everett }
Israel Blagg }

Israel Blagg only on his trial

Jury Sworn, Number One, who returned the following Verdict, to wit.

Not Guilty.

                                        Richard D. Gray, foreman

---

James Hargrave, in   }
right of his wife, app.l }
vs   }
Samuel McKie   }
William McKie, Resp.ts }

A rule having been obtained in this Case at April term last, for the Respondent to Shew Cause why the appeal should not be entered Nunce pro tune. No cause being shewn at this term, and on Motion of Appellant's Counsel. It is ordered, that the Said appeal be allowed to be entered now for then. Whereupon, James Hargrove came into Court and entered himself appellant in the place of Henry Parks.

Teste. Maxfield H. Payne, Clk   James Hargrove

The State   }   vs
} Ind^t Assault
Winkfield Bagwell }

We, the Jury, find the Prisoner guilty.

                                         R. D. Gray, forman

The State   }   vs
} Ind^t Assault
Cleverly Philips } fined five

dollars & the cost.

The Court then adjourned untill to morrow morning Eight O'Clock.

Test. Maxfield H. Payne, Clk

Ex^d Young Gresham
The Court met on Thursday 13th October 1814 according to adjournment. present

his honor Judge Gresham.

~~Georgia } Franklin County } To the honorable Superior Court for the County.~~

~~The Petition of Jane Robertson, widow and relict of William Robertson, late of Said County, deceased, humbly Sheweth, That the Said Wm Robertson, Dec^d, the late husband of your petitioner was in his lifetime and at the time of his death~~

Franklin Superior Court

Upon the Petition of Jane Robertson, relict & widow of Wm Robertson, Dec^d, Stating that she is entitled to her third part or dower in and to a tract of land Containing 287½ Acres Granted to Joseph Wise and also one other tract containing 226 acres Granted to said Wm Robertson adjoining each other and Situate, lying, & being on the Hudson fork of Broad river in said County, of which Said Several tracts of lands the said Wm Robertson lately died Seized. Therefore, Ordered that Hezekiah Terrell, the Sheriff of Said County, James Ramsey, Samuel McKie, William Ash, Henry Parks, Thomas Mays, William Thomas, John Clarkson, Joshua Hudson, Gabril Martin, James McCarty, and James Allan repair to the residence of the late Wm Robertson and then and there apportion, lay off, and Set apart by proper metes and bounds the dower or third part of the said several tracts of land including the mansion house and deliver possession thereof to the said Jane Robertson, paying due regard to the quantity and quality of said lands. And, after having performed the duty required of them, the said partitioners will certify & return a correct plat of the same under their hands & Seals and deposit the Same in the Clerk's Office

___ of this Court within three months

hereafter.

Petit Jury N° 1
    1. Jesse Putman   7. Peter Brown
    2. Robert Harrisson   8. Wm Eddins
    3. John Clarkson   9. George Taylor
    4. Joel Hunt   10. James Mitchell
    5. Archabald Cogburn   11. James Mercer
    6. Jacob Redwine   12. John Temples

The State   }
    vs   } Ind^t Trespass
David B. Manly }

True Bill.   Fred^k Beall, Forman
The State   }   vs
} Ind^t Assault
Darby Thompson }

True Bill.   Fred^k Beall, Forman

The State   }
    vs   } Ind^t Taking & inveigling a letter from Post office
William Cawthon }
David Reed &   }
Larkin Cawthon }

True Bill against William Cowthon & Larkin Cowthon.   Fred^k Beall, Forman

The State   }   vs
} Ind^t Bastardy
Chiswell McDaniel }

No Bill.   F. Beall, Form^n

___

The State } vs } Ind^t misdemeanor
Wm A. Blackburn }

Nol pros on account of the words "this State" being left out in the bill.

The State } vs
} Ind^t Perjury
Peter Wagner }
True Bill.   Fred^k Beall, Form^n

The State }
    vs   } Ind^t Misdemeanor
Wm Ramsey }
True Bill.   Fred^k Beall, Form^n

The State }
    vs   } Ind^t Petit Larceny
John Everett }
Israel Blagg }

True Bill.   Fred^k Beall, Form^n

The State }
vs   } Ind^t Assault
Wm Ramsey }
True Bill.   Fred^k Beall, Form^n

James Lowell }
    vs   } Trespass on the Case
Joseph Chandler }

Jury N° 1 as at first

We, the Jury, find for the Plaintiff fifty dollars, with Cost of Suit.

                                   R. D. Gray, forman

Franklin Superior Court

Upon the petition of Maxfield H. Payne, in right of his wife Sarah, formerly Sarah Williamson, relict & Widow of Wm Williamson, Dec^d, Stating that he is entitled in right of his Wife to her third part or dower in and to a tract of land containing Six hundred Sixty two & an half acre, Granted to Lewis Bobo & Ralph Banks, adjoining lands of F. Beall, H. Terrell, & Mathews, lying on Stephens Creek in Said County, of which said tract of land the Said Wm Williamson lately died Seized.

Therefore Ordered, that Hezekiah Terrell, Esqr, Sheriff of Said County, Fred^k Beall, Benj^a Dorsey, George King, John R. Brown, James Williamson, John Williamson, W. F. Bagwell, Thomas Payne, Adam Cloud, Charles Rice, and Samuel Williamson repair to the residence of the late Wm Williamson, Dec^d, and then & there apportion, lay off, and Set apart, by proper metes and bounds, the dower or third part of the Said tract of land, including the mansion house, if any, and deliver possession thereof to the Said

Maxfield H. Payne in right of his wife, paying due regard to the quantity & quality of Said land.

And after performing the duty required of them, the Said partitioners will Certify & return a correct plat of the Same, under their hands & Seals, & deposit the Same in the Clerk's office of this Court on or before the first day of the next Term.

         James Smith, Atto for petitioner

Richard Smith, }
Ex Demise of } Robert
Barnwell }
 vs   } Ejectment
William Stiles } &
Others }

I appear for the defendants and hereby Confess a Judgment in favour of the plaintiff for the premises in dispute, with the priviledge of an appeal as if there was a verdict in favour of the Said plaintiffs, and Costs of Suit.
13th Octr 1814   Walton Harris, Defts' Atty

The State   } vs
} Ind^t assault
Farley Thompson }

Samuel Tate, who was Surety of the defendant in the above case, delivered up the said defendant & there upon was discharged.

Joseph Embry & others }
Caviators   }
 vs   } appeal from the Inferior Court
The Executors of }
Joseph Glenn, Dec^d }

Special Jury Sworn

1. James Allan 7. Redfearn Wims
2. Wm Jones   8. Abner Dunnigan
3. Jno Warmock 9. Darby Henley
4. Robt Barnhill 10. Moses Sanders
5. Joseph Watters 11. Reuben Shotwell
6. Meredith Brown 12. Charles Rice

We, the Jury, Say that the Testator was Sane at the time of Signing the will and that the will was not obtained by unlawful means.

             James Allan, Form^n

Franklin Superior Court

Upon the Petition of John Haynes in right of his wife Sarah, Wm Robins in right of his wife Mary, & John Hollingsworth, three of the heirs of Saml Hollingsworth, Dec^d, Stating that they are entitled to their distributive Shares of a tract of land, of which Said Saml Hollingsworth died possessed of, Containing five hundred Acres, more or less, Situate, lying, & being in Said County, on the Grove fork of Broad river, Granted to Peter B. Terrell, adjoining lands of Moses Sanders, Thomas Neel, John Hill, & Richd Maulders.

being one sixth equal share. Therefore, it is ordered, that Hezekiah Terrell, Esqr, high Sheriff of said County, John Baugh, Darby Henly, William Bush, Samuel Haiden, Joseph Payne, William Walraven, Reuben Shotwell, Edmund King, J^r, Aries Cox, Richard Malden, and Robert Malone repair to the residence of the said Samuel Hollingsworth, late of said County, deceased, and then and there apportion, lay off, and set apart, by proper metes and bounds, the sixth equal share of said tract of land to the said John Haynes in right of his wife, Wm Robbin in right of his wife, and John Hollingsworth, having due regard to quantity and quallity, and that the Clerk issue a Writ of Partition directed to the above named persons accordingly. And, after having performed the duty required of them in this regard, they will deliver possession thereof to said heirs respectively and make out a correct plat of their proceedings and deposit the same in the Clerk's

Office of this Court, on or before the first day of the next term.

13th Oct 1814　　　　　　　　　　　　　　James Smith
　　　　　　　　　　　　　　　　　　　　　applicant's Attorney

The Court then adjourned untill tomorrow morning Nine O'Clock.

Test. Maxfield H. Payne, Clk

Ex^d　　　　　　　　　　　　　　　　　Young Gresham

The Court met According to adjournment on friday the 14th of October 1814.

The admr^s of Amos Bratcher, app^s }
　　vs　　　　　　　　　　　　　　} Trover
Stephen Westbrook, resp^t　　　　}

Superior Court Verdict at Oct Term 1814

On motion of counsel of appellants, it is ordered that the respondent show cause on the first day of the next Term, or so soon thereafter as counsel can be heard, why a new trial should not be had on the said case on the following grounds.

1st Because the said verdict is contrary to evidence & the principles of justice & Equity.

2nd Because the Court admitted in evidence on the part of Resp^t a bill of sale for the negro in dispute from Barbara Moss & Amos Bratchers dated in 1800 to the said Resp^t, the said Barbara being then

———

the person under & from whom the said admr^s claim title by Bill of Sale, and the said Amos one of the said admrs and a son of the intestate of of the appellants; which bill of sale purported to have been made long anterior to the date of the said administration. 3rd Because it was proved that at the time of the said Bill of sale purported to have been made, there was one other distribution of the estate of Amos Bratcher, the intestate, to wit, Nancy Bratcher, who intermarried with Whitaker, who was no party to the Said Bill of Sale, and who lived Several years after the date thereof, and that therefore, if the said Amos as a distributor could even legally Convey a right, he could transfer a moiety only of & to the said Negro.

4th Because a Distributee, especially where there are more than one before distribution, cannot legally convey an interest in or title to personalty, so as to deprive admr^s of their right to recover property which was of the Estate of the intestate, the ancestor of such Distributor.

5th because the Court expressed a decided opinion that Barbara Moss could transfer no right by her Bill of Sale to respondent having in 1788 by the name of Barbara Richardson Conveyed all her right to the Negro in dispute by Bill of Sale under her hand and Seal to the intestate of the said Admr^s.

6th Because it was left doubtful and indifferent by the Respondent's own evidence whether the Said Amos Bratcher, under whom the said respondent claims Title by the said Bill of Sale made in 1800, was not illegemate child, and if so clearly not entitled Distribute of the said Intestate.

7th Because the Jury found generally for respondent, when even Suffering that the Said Bill of Sale dated in 1800 was legal evidence in the Said cause and that the Said A. Bratcher Could by the Said Bill of Sale to respondent transfer an interest of ward to the

———

Said Negroe as Distribution before Distribution & before administration Granted. The respondent shewed no title whatever, but a Moiety of the Said Negro, who was proved to be of the value of $500 and his hire for 10 years to be of the value of $20 p^r annum. 8th That the Said verdict is Contrary to Law.

9th That the Said Bill of Sale dated in 1800 ought to have been pleaded. By not pleading the Said Bill of Sale, the Said admr^s were Surprised, especially as they were lead to believe that the Respondent meant to rely upon a release from the Said Amos Bracher, as adm^r of Amos Bracher, the Intestate of the Said Amos.

Petit Jury N° 1

1. Jesse Putman
2. Robert Harrison
3. John Gober
4. Joel Hunt
5. Arch^d Cogburn
6. Jacob Redwine
7. Peter Brown
8. Wm Eddins
9. George Taylor
10. ~~James Mitchell~~ Richd D. Gray
11. James Mercer
12. John Temples

William Chisolm }
    vs   } Atta
Charles Paine   }

Rhoda Cawthon, Summoned and deposed as a Garnishee in this Case and the Oath of the Garnishee traversed. It being admitted in this Case that the levy of the above attachment was made on the property of Wm Cawthon, deceased, who died intestate, before administration Granted on the estate of the Said William Cawthon,

———

under Just circumstances, the Court doth adjudge & determine that the Said Garnishee Could not be legally Summoned, that the oath of the Garnishee is correct, and that the Said Garnishee be & She is hereby discharged. But the Judgment against the absconding debtor is not by this decision to be considered as in any wise invalidated.

Christopher Lowry }
    vs   } Trespass vi et armis
Winkfield Bagwell }

Jury N° 1

We, the Jury, find for the Plaintiff Eighty dollars, with Costs of Suit.

                                                      R. D. Gray, forman

The Adm^r of A. Bratcher }
    vs   } Trover verdict for Dft and
Stephen Westbrooks   } Rule Nisi for new Trial

The Counsels for the admr^s of A. Bratcher Shewing to the Court that Richard Woods is a material Witness for them in the Trial of the Said cause, that he is old and infirm, and that they fear the Said Richard will depart this life before they can produce rugarlarly the Testimony of the Said Richard in the event of A new trial being Granted, for which A rule nisi is Granted & pending. Whereupon, is ordered that the Said admr^s have leave to take

———

Examination of the Said Richard in the usual way, by commission & interrogatories, Serving the Same Stephen or his attorney with A copy or copies thereof, provided that the act of the General assembly in Such cases made & provided be Strictly pursued.

Lemuel J. Alston, } plaintiff in
Execution, }
Appellant } vs }
Robert Malone, }
Claimant Resp^t }

Special Jury Sworn.

1. James Allan	7. Adam Whisenhunt
2. Thos Payne	8. Meredith Brown
3. John Mayfield	9. Redfearn Wims
4. John Warmack	10. Abner Dunnigan
5. Robert Barnhill	11. Reuben Shotwell
6. Joseph Walters	12. Charles Rice

We, the Jury, Say the negro is not Subject to the execution.

James Allan, Form^n

The State } vs } Ind^t Misdemeanor
Wm A. Blackburn }
No Bill.   Fred^k Beall, Form^n

Jesse Putman }
     vs   } Assault & Battery
David Allison }

Settled at Deft's Cost.

———

Grand Jurors drawn for April Term 1815

1. Esaias Harboin	19. James Sewell
2. James Denmore	20. John Stubbs
3. George Cockburn	21. Levi Garrisson
4. Russell Jones	22. William Robins
5. James R. Wyly	23. Martin Sims
6. Henry Parks	24. John McNeel
7. John Payne, Senr	25. James Riley
8. John Baugh	26. William Wood
9. John E. Carson	27. Thomas Newton
10. Simon Terrell	28. Banj^a Cleveland, Ma^j
11. Martin Herndin	29. Sampson Lane
12. Neely Dobson	30. Joseph Chandler, gum log
13. John Stonecypher	31. Joel Yowell
14. Joseph Martin	32. John Bush
15. Joseph Morris	33. Winkf^d Bagwell

16. Joseph Terrell
17. John Morris
18. John McEntire

34. William Hackett
35. George Stovall, J^r
36. Joshua Hudson

Benjamin Rogers & Co }
    vs   } Debt
Dudley Jones   }

Dismissed at Defendant's Cost.

___

Petit Jurors drawn for April Term

1. Moses Walters
2. Robt Fleming
3. Richd Bond, Senr
4. John Barton
5. John Sewell
6. Major Neel
7. George Gober

8. Jacob Garner
9. John Ayers
10. John Bowman
11. William Tucker
12. Mathew McCarter
13. Green Sewell
14. Willm Wilkerson
15. John Coil
16. Chesley Cawthon
17. George Rucker, Senr
18. Jonathan Baugh
19. Charles Isam
20. John Ash
21. John Crump
22. W^m McCracken
23. William Ash
24. Jesse Brawner
25. Thomas Hill
26. James Jordan
27. John Brown
28. Wm Terrell
29. Henry Avery
30. Benj^a Cleveland
31. Benj^a Love
32. James Armstrong

33. William Bole
34. Jesse Smith
35. Edmund Strange
36. Charles Tracey
37. Thomas Cox
38. David Anthony
39. Hugh B. Greenwood
40. Jesse Blackwell
41. Saml Burton
42. Reuben Warren
43. David Mitchell
44. James Henderson
45. Jeremiah Sparks
46. Thomas Morgan
47. Beall Baker
48. John Meadows

Georgia }
Franklin County } We, the Grand Jury for the County aforesaid, October Term 1814, do present our Thanks to his honor Young Gresham for his due attention during said Term in keeping Good order and Expediting the Business the came before him while Sitting as a Court.

We have also the pleasure to observe that we have no presentments to return.

Oct. 14, 1814 F. Beall, F^m

The Court adjourned untill to morrow morning Eight O'Clock.

Test. Maxfield H. Payne, Clk

Ex^d Young Gresham

The Court met according to adjournment on Saturday the 15th October 1814. Present, his Honor Judge Gresham.

~~The Court then adjourned until Court in course.~~

Wm Chisolm }
    vs } Traverse of Garnishee's Affidavit & dismissed
Rhoda Cawthon, Garnishee }

On motion, of J. Smith, Plffs Atty, it is ordered that the Garnishee Shew Cause on the first day of the next Term, or as soon thereafter as Counsel can be heard, why the above Case Should not be reinstated on the following Grounds.

1st That the distributive Share of Charles Payne was legally attached.

2nd That the adm^{rs} may be compelled by law to depose what she hath in hand belonging to Such distribute after debts are paid or that was in hand at the time of the levy of the attachment at any time after the levy & before deposition.

3rd That the circumstance of the Garnishee having administered after levy of attachment ought not to prejudice the right of a creditor, but that the Same is legally bound to answer the demand of Plff in attachment.

The Court then adjourned untill Court in Course.

Test. Maxfield H. Payne, Clk

Ex^d Young Gresham

Benjamin Dorsey }
    vs   } Judgment
Dudley Jones   }

In the above Case, the Defendant, being dissatisfied with the Verdict, Came into Office, and with him also Came Fred^k Beall, his Security, and acknowledged them Selves bound for the eventual Condemnation money and Costs, pays up the Cost & prays an appeal. In witness whereof we have Set our hands and Seals, this 17th day of October 1814.

Test. Maxfield H. Payne, Clk   Dudley Jones, Fred^k Beall

Joseph Hamilton, appellant   }
    vs   } Case in nature of Deceipt
William Thompson, Respondent }

William Cawthon }
    vs   } Attachment
William Paine   }

Settled & Cost paid.

April Term 1815

The Superior Court of Franklin County met on the tenth day, being the Second monday in April 1815.

Present, His Honor Judge Gresham.

According to the exegiance of a Writ of Venire to him directed, the high Sheriff of said County returned said writ with the following persons Summoned & Sworn as Grand Jurors, Viz.

    1. Sampson Lane   13. John Baugh

    2. John Stonecypher   14. Joseph Terrell

    3. Joseph Morris   15. Wm Robins

    4. James Sewell   16. John McIntyre

    5. John Stubbs   17. Joel Yowell

    6. Levi Garrison   18. Wm Hackett

    7. John McNeel   19. James R. Wyly

    8. Wm Ward   20. John Morris

      9. Joseph Chandler   21. Henry Parks

10. George Stovall   22. John Payne, Senr
11. Neely Dobson
12. John E. Carson

———

April Term 1815

Petit Jury N° 1

    1. Robert Fleming   7. ~~Green Berry Sewell~~ William Bole
    2. Richard Bond, Se^r   8. Chesley Cawthon
    3. John Sewell   9. ~~Henry Avery~~ James Henderson
    4. John Ayers   10. John Crump
    5. John Bowman   11. Thomas Hill
    6. Mathew McCarter   12. Jesse Brawner

The State   }
    vs   } Ind^t assault
Wyatt Brown }

True Bill.   Sampson Lane, foreman

The State   }   vs
} Ind^t murder
Joseph Edwards }

True Bill.   Sampson Lane, foreman

The Court then adjourned untill to morrow morning Nine O'Clock.
Test. Maxfield H. Payne, Clk

Ex^d   Young Gresham

The Court met According to adjournment on tuesday the 11th April 1815.

Present, his honor Judge Gresham.

———

April Term 1815

John Temples)
    vs   } Case
Moses Parnell }

Jury N° 1

We, the Jury, find for the plaintiff one hundred and fifty Dollars, with Cost.
                                                        William Bole, foreman

Petit Jury N⁰ 1

1. Robert Fleming
2. Richard Bond, Se^r
3. John Sewell
4. John Ayers
5. Benj^a Cleveland
6. Mathew McCarter
7. William Bole
8. Chesley Cawthon
9. Henry Avery
10. John Crump
11. Thomas Hill
12. Jesse Brawner

John doe, ex dem }
John Bowman }
    vs }
John A. Verdel }
& Ja^s Tait }

nonsuit.

Robert Chandler }
    vs } Libel for a Divorce
Janes Chandler }

1. John Stonecypher
2. Joseph Morris
3. John Stubbs
4. Wm Ward
5. John McNeal
6. George Stovall
7. Joseph Terrell
8. Wm Robins
9. John McIntyre
10. Wm Hackett
11. John E. Carson
12. John Paine, Senr

We, the Jury, find that Sufficient proofs have been offered to our consideration to a ___ authorize a total divorce, that is to say, a Divorce a Vinculo matrimonie, upon legal principles between the parties in this Case.

                                        John E. Carson, fm

Elijah Sparks }
    vs } Deceit Franklin
Charles Worel }

The parties, being desirous to Settle this dispute in the above case, have agreed to Submit the matter to the arbitration of John Morris, ~~Joel Yowell~~, Joseph Chandler, John Stonecypher, & David Morgan, who are to choose a fifth person, to provide & if those named Should not agree, he is to vote & decide the Same as Umpire, which agreement being made Known to the Court. It is Ordered, that the Said Arbitrators [faint] as soon convenient after reasonable notice to all parties concerned & hear the Evidence from Each Side, & make out their award a [illegible] prescribed from under their hands & Seals, which being returned to next Term of this Court shall be made the Judgment of Said Court, & that the Clerk issue a Copy of this Rule to either party on application & deliver the papers in Office relative to said case which are to be returned with the award.

            Charles Worel, Elijah Sparks

The State } vs
} Ind^t assault
Thomas Payne }
& James Reid }

True Bill.   Sampson Lane, foreman

James Ward }
 vs } Trover
Bryan Ward }

Saml Ward }
vs } Trover
Joseph Martin }

Saml Ward }
vs } Trover
Jno Lane, Junr }

The above Cases Settled at the Costs of Plaintiff, who is in addition to the usual Court Costs to pay the Witnesses summoned in the Said Cases by the Defendants to be included in the Bills of Costs and execution therefore may issue against the plaintiff for the same.

Henry Avery, being one of the Petit Jury Summoned and empaneled at the present Term & appearing on the Jury So much intoxicated as to disqualify him from discharging his duty. it is ordered, that he pay a fine of thirty dollars for a Contempt of this Court & that he remain in Safe Custody untill the fine is paid.

William Scott }
 vs } Trover
William Goodwin }

Nonsuit.

Alexander Williamson, appellant }
    vs   } Replogle
Charity Woodall, Respondant }

Abated by death of the appellant.

William H. Hall }
    vs   } Case
Robert Brien }

Settled at plffs Cost.

Samuel Ward }
    vs   } Trover
Bryan Martin }

Settled at plffs Costs.

Samuel Ward }
    vs   } Trover
Joseph Martin }

Settled at plffs Costs.

Samuel Ward }
    vs   } Trover
John Lane, J^r }

Settled at plffs Costs.

Georgia, Hancock Superior Court, August Term 1814 Rules & orders passed at the Term aforesaid. 1st All appeals hereafter Granted Shall be entered on the minutes of the Court, & no appeal Shall be held as Valid and properly entered, unless entered by the party himself, or his attorney at Law concerned in the Suit, or some person having a power or authority in writing to act for Said party and any appeal not So entered Shall be dismissed on motion, if such motion be made at the first Term after the entry of Said appeal, and in case no motion for dismissal of Said appeal be made at the Said first Term, the appeal Shall be considered as properly entered.

2nd that the Clerks of the Superior Courts of this circuit Shall keep a motion Docket on which it Shall be their duty to enter all motions made to the Court in the order in which they are made, the names of the parties to Such motion & the attorneys concerned in the Same, which motions Shall be argued in order.

It is further ordered that the Clerk

of this Court do forthwith transmit a Copy of these rules to each Clerk of the Superior Courts in this Circuit.

Taken from the Minutes.   Phil. L. Simms, Clk

The Court then adjourned untill to morrow morning Nine O'Clock.

Test. Maxfield H. Payne, Clk

Ex^d Young Gresham

The Court met according to adjournment on Wednesday 12th April 1815.

Present, his Honor Judge Gresham.

Henry Avery, who was find yesterday thirty dollars, having made his excuse this morning and it appearing Satisfactory, thereupon the find is remitted.

James Hargroves }
& Wife   }
     vs   } Bill in Equity
Samuel McKie   }
W^m McKie   }

Nonsuit.

Edmund King   } Franklin Superior Court vs }
In Equity
Samuel Phillips }
Edmond Henley   }
William Henley }
Jane Henley   }
Mary Henley   }

In this case, a rule having been obtained at April Term 1814 of this Honorable Court, Stating that the complainant having obtained leave to amend his Bill, & the amended Bill having been Served, & not answered. It was then ordered, that the respondants Served in the amended bill answer in thirty days or the Bill be taken pro confeso.

and now at this Term, it appearing that the defendants have not answered, according to the Terms of Said Rule, on motion of counsel for the Complainant. It is ordered, that the said amended Bill be & is taken as for confessed as to all the facts & charges therein contained.

Isaac J. Barrett }
      vs   } Trespass
Farley Thompson   }

Jury N º 1

We, the Jury, find for the plaintiff One hundred and fifty dollars, with Cost of Suit.

William Bole, forman

James Hobson }
vs } Libel for a Divorce Sarah Hobson }

Special Jury as in the other.

we, the Jury, find Sufficient proofs have been refered to our consideration to authorize a total divorce, that is to say, a Divorce a Vinculo matrimonie upon legal principles between the parties in the Case.

John E. Carson, fm

Richard Harrison }
plff in Execution }
      vs   }
Ambrous Blackburn }
Claiment }

Settled.

The State } vs
} Ind^t assault
Alexander Talbert }
True Bill.

Sampson Lane, fm

The State }
   vs } Ind^t murder
Joseph Edwards }

    1. Robert Fleming   7. Drury Rose
    2. Richard Bond, Se^r 8. Samuel McKie
    3. Major Neal   9. James Hulsey
    4. James Tate   10. Richard Gray
    5. Thomas Morgan   11. Benj^a ~~Adrine~~ Whitehead
    6. John Nail   12. Fleming Adrine

We, the Jury, find the prisoner at the Bar guilty of the offence of man Slaughter on the within indictment.

James Tate, F. M.

The Court then adjourned untill to morrow morning Nine O'Clock.

Test. Maxfield H. Payne, Clk

Ex^d   Young Gresham

The Court met according to adjournment On thursday the 13th April 1815.

Present, his Honor Judge Gresham.

John Payne   }
vs   } Certiorari
John Williams }

certiorari Sustained & proceedings in the Justices Court set aside so far as regards the Verdict of the Jury & a further trial to be had before a Second Jury.

Franklin Superior Court April Term 1815. We, the Grand Inquest of said County, 1st Present to his Honor Judge Gresham our Sincere thanks for his unremitted and Constant attention in preserving Good order & the faithful Discharge of the duties Incumbent on him during the present Term.

2nd We present as a Grievance the present State of our County Funds, as it appears from the Books in the Clerk's Office of the Inferior Court of this County,

---

that a number of the Justices of the peace has faild to account with the Clerke of the Office aforesaid for the Money or monies arising from the Sales of Estrays and Recommend Such measures to be taken as may compel them to a Discharge of their duty. 3rd We present as a Grievance the bad & almost intire Neglected Situation of our roads in General, and earnestly recommend that that Commissioners and Overseers of the Roads aforesaid will exert the powers vested in them by law for the immediate repairing of the Same.

4th We view with extreme regret the agitation of the public mind, excited by the disagreement of Opinion in the Different departments of State, we earnestly receommend ~~that~~ that the public fever may abate, that opposition may be quieted, and that all classes may unite with gratefull, Gladsong, Hearts in Hailing the return of peace, and the unrestrained administration of Justice.

5th We view with extreme regret that so little attention is paid to those morral principles that should be promoted in all republican Governments, and presents as a grievance the frequent practice of Gambling in this County, especially in the Villedge of Carnesville

Carnesville.

    1. Sampson Lane, foreman

John Stonecypher	John Baugh
Joseph Morris	Joseph Terrell
James Sewell	Wm Robins
John Stubbs	John McIntire
Levi Garrison	Joel Yowell
John McNeal	Wm Hackett
Wm Ward	James R. Wyley
Joseph Chandler	John Morris
George Stovall	Henry Parks

Neely Dobson   John E.   John Payne, Senr
Carson

N. B. We Recommend that these presentments be published Once in the Athens Gazette.

The Court then took up the presentments & ordered them to be published pursuant to their request.

The Court then adjourned untill to morrow morning Eight O'Clock.

Ex^d Young Gresham

Test. Maxfield H. Payne

The Court met according to adjournment friday the 14th April 1815.

Present, His Honor Judge Gresham.

~~The State~~   }   vs
} ~~Ind^t murder~~
~~Joseph Edwards~~ }

Georgia   }
Franklin County } I, Green W. Smith, do solemnly Swear that I will well and truly demean myself as Attorney, Solicitor, and Proctor in the several Courts of Law and Equity in this State, that I will maintain, support, & defend the Constitution of this State & the Constitution of the United States. So help me God.

Sworn to in open Court   Green W. Smith
13th April 1815

Test. Maxfield H. Payne, Clk

On Petition of Green W. Smith praying to be examined Concerning his Service on Law, and if found competent, to be permitted to practice & plead in the several Courts in this State. this day being assigned, he was interrogated in open Court, and the Court being Satisfied as well of the Moral Character as well as to the Capacity of the applicant, and the usual oath being administered, & entered on record. It is ordered, that Green W. Smith be and he is hereby authorized to plead & practice in the several Courts of Law and equity in this State agreeably to the Statute in such Cases made & provided. 13th April 1815

Grand Jurors drawn forOcto^r 1815

1. James Martin, Esq.
2. Meredith Brown
3. Josiah Stovall
4. Isaac J. Barrett
5. Stephen Poe
6. Wm Bush
7. Thompson Moore
8. John D. Terrell
9. Chris Baker
10. Robert Neel
11. Benj^a Dorsey
12. John R. Brown
13. James Hooper
14. Littleton Meeks
15. James Bleur
16. John Selman
17. Aaron Campbell
18. Saml Ferguson, Esq
19. Abner Dunnagin
20. James McDonald
21. Epps Chatham
22. John Nail
23. Saml Shannon
24. John Trimble
25. Ben^j Starritt
26. Wm Jones, Esq.
27. James Ramsey, H. R.
28. Richd Wood
29. James Hulsey, Senr
30. Thos Hollingsworth
31. Edwd Leavell
32. Gabriel Martin
33. John Sanders, J^r
34. W^m [faint] Senr
35. Edm^d Henley
36. Edm^d King, Senr

Petit Jurors

1. David Ford
2. Thomas Neal
3. Reuben Bramblett
4. James Starrett
5. Wm Glover
6. Clem^t Walters
7. Jesse Holland, Junr
8. Richd Carns
9. George Barger
10. John Purcell
11. Austin Kendrick
12. John Askew
13. Stephen Westbrook
14. Squire Markham
15. Fred^k Braswell
16. Aris Cox
17. Ob. Ayers
18. John Baker
19. Thomas Gazoway
20. John Dorsey

---

21. William Holbrooks
22. Jeremiah Milner
34. Wm Becker B. Smith
35. Zach Tabar

23. John Campbell
24. Richd Wood, J^r
25. Owen Andrews
26. James Lowrey
27. James Flood
28. Joseph Reed
29. Arch McGrady
30. James Jones
31. Wm Blackwell
32. Thos Clark, Senr
33. Thos Anderson

36. David Thornton
37. Elijah Walters
38. Aaron Tilman
39. Saml Brazer
40. Thomas Carns
41. John Smith
42. James Jones
43. Wm Wofford
44. Wm Caruth
45. Saml Post
46. Wilson Howington
47. Allen Chandler
48. Elisha Ashworth

Drawn in Open Court.

John Troy, for } the use of
Wm Samson }
vs } Trespass on the Case Georgia Sherell }

On Motion of Counsell for the plaintiff, it is ordered that the defendant Shew cause on the first day of the next Term, or so Soon thereafter as counsel can be heard, why the nonsuit in the above case should not be Set aside & the case be reinstated on the docket, on the Ground that the nonsuit was entered in consequence of the absence of the plaintiff's Attorney with the papers necessary for the prosecution of the Case.

The State }
    vs } Indict Murder
Joseph Edwards } Verdict Manslaughter

It is ordered by the Court, that Joseph Edwards appear on the Wednesday of the next term of this Court, between the Hours of 10 O'Clock in the forenoon & five O'Clock in the afternoon of that day, and then at the bar of this Court you are to be branded in the brawr of the left Thumb with a hot Iron by the proper Officer with the letter M and thence to be discharged on the Payments of Costs, in the Mean time you are to give ample Security in the penalty of five thousand Dollars for your appearance at the day above named to receive the Sentence of the Court hereupon named.

The State }
vs } Sci fa W^m
Ayers & }
Garland Ayers }

Ju^r N° 1

We, the Jury, find against William Ayers the sum of two hundred dollars as principal in the recognizance & againsts Garland the sum of one hundred dollars as Security.

Wm Bole, f. m.

The State }
vs } Sci fa
Baker Ayers, Junr }

Jury N° 1

We, the Jury, find for the plaintiff the sum of two hundred dollars against Baker Ayers principal in the recognizance & the Sum of one hundred dollars as Security & Cost.

William B. Wofford, administrator }
vs } Case
Hudson Moss & }
Garland lane }

Settled. ~~nonsuit.~~

Heirs of Peter Williamson }
vs } Bill in Equity and award returned at
Edmund King & } October Term 1813
Elizabeth King, }
Ex^r & Exr^x of P. Williamson }

The parties in this Case, having agreed in open Court that the award which was returned and lost, was returned in favor of the Heirs of Peter Williamson against the above defendants. It is ordered that the plaintiff's attorney be allowed to enter up Judgment for the Sum of three hundred dollars, the Sum agreed to by the parties.

The Adm^rs of Thomas Carter, dec^d }
vs } Sci fa
The Administration of John Gorham, dec^d }

April Term 1815

The above Sci fa having been issued, Calling upon Edmund Henley, administrator of John Gorham, deceased, to Shew Cause why Thomas S. Carter & Charles Carter, administrators of Thomas Carter, deceased, Should not be made parties to Said execution, & the Judgment be revived, & execution issue in the name of the said administrators of Thomas Carter, deceased, & no Sufficient Cause being Shewn. It is ordered & considered by the court, that the Judgment in the said Scire facias mentioned be revived, & that the said Thomas S. Carter & Charles Carter, administrators of Thomas Carter, deceased. have their execution against the said Edmund Henley, administrators of John Gorham, deceased, for the debt & damages in the said Judgment in the said Scire facias named mentioned according to the form & effect thereof, that is to Say, for the Sum of twelve hundred dollars, with interest thereon, to be Calculated from the Eleventh day of April in the year eighteen hundred, together with the further sum of twenty Seven dollars in that action recovered for Costs, and also the further sum of [blank] for their costs in this behalf laid out & expended, & that the said Thomas S. Carter & Charles Carter may likewise

———

have execution thereof, & the said Edmund in mercy &C.

The Court then adjourned untill Court in Course.

Test. Maxfield H. Payne, Clk

Ex^d Young Gresham

Isaac J. Barrett }
     vs   } Verdict & Ind^t April Term 1815
Farley Thompson }

This day came the defendant Farley Thompson into office Benjamin Starritt and Thomas Wilkins, his Securities, the said defendant being dissatisfied with the verdict & having paid the Cost, and prays an appeal, and the said Farley Thompson & his securities, Benjamin Starritt & Thomas Wilkins, acknowledge themselves bound to the plaintiff to the plaintiff Isaac J. Barrett for the eventual Condemnation money and Cost in terms of the Cost.

Given under our hands & seals   Farley Thompson
This 14th April 1815   B. Starritt
                                       Thomas X Wilkins, his mark

Test. Maxfield H. Payne, Clk

———

October Term 1815

The Superior Court of Franklin County was Called and adjourned on the Second monday in said month October by Directions from his Honor Judge Gresham for that purpose, the Judge being unable to attend, which adjournment was untill the first monday in December, at which time his honor the Judge met agreeable to adjournment. December 4th 1815

According to the exegeince of a Writ of Venire to him directed, the high Sheriff of Said County returned said Writ, with the following persons Summoned & Sworn as Grand Jurors, Viz.

    1. John R. Brown   12. Thos Hollingsworth
    2. Meredith Brown   13. Edmund Henley
    3. Thompson Moore   14. Edmund King, S^r
    4. Christopher Baker   15. Isaac J. Barrett
    5. Robert Neal   16. Wm Jones, Esqr
    6. James Hooper   17. Stephen Poe
    7. James McDonald   18. Richd Gray

8. John Nail
9. John Trimble
10. James Ramsey
11. James Hulsey, Senr
19. Joseph Chandler
20. Josiah Stovall
21. Ben^j Starrett
22. James Martin, Sn^r
23. Wm Burk

October Term 1815

The Solicitor General failing to attend, it is ordered by the Court, that Edmund Paine, Esquire, be & he is hereby appointed Solicitor General pro tempore.

Petit Jury N° 1

1. ~~Squire Markham~~ Absalom Baker
2. Fred^k Braszell
3. Obediah Ayers
4. John Baker
5. John Dorsey
6. William Holbrook
7. John Campbell
8. Owen Anders
9. Joseph Reed
10. James Jones
11. Wm Blackwell
12. Thos Clark

Thomas Ivy }
vs } Case Bail
Robert Milton }

in this Case, Aron Strickland, the Bail ~~in this Case~~, delivered up the Defendant, Robert Milton, into Court and thereupon was discharged. and Adam Shuffield acknowledges himself Bound as Bail in the Room & Stead of the said Aron Strickland. Test. Maxfield H. Payne, Clk Adam X Shuffield, his mark

The Court then adjourned untill tomorrow morning Nine O'Clock.

Test. Maxfield H. Payne, Clk

October Term 1815

The Court met on Tuesday morning, being the fifth day of December 1815, according to adjournment.

Test. Maxfield H. Payne, Clk
Ex^d Young Gresham

Jury N° 1

1. Fred^k Braszel
2. Obediah Ayers
3. John Baker
4. William Holbrook
7. James Jones
8. Wm Blackwell
9. Thos Clark
10. James Starrett

   5. John Campbell   11. Aris Cox
   6. Joseph Reed   12. Thos Carnes

Elijah Sparks }
 vs   } Deceipt
Charles Word }

the award returned & made the Judgment of the Court.

Thomas D. Jordan }
  vs   } Debt
John D. Terrell & } G.
D. Paine   }

John D. Terrell Served.

By consent of parties, it is agreed to refer all matters of difference in the said Case to the award & final determination of Joseph Chandler, Joel Yowel, Robert Hackett, and John Brice, with the liberty of calling in an umpire, whose award to be final in the said Case, provided the same be made in Ten Days and in writing, signed by the said arbitrators, or a majority of them, or umpire, both parties to have notice of the time & place of the meeting of the said arbitrators or umpire for the purpose

---

<u>October Term 1815</u>

of making an award.

Moses Fleming }
vs } Trespass for meachprofits Adam Shuffield }

Dismissed at Defts Cost.

Pettit Jury N° 2
   1. Aris Cox   7. William Martin
   2. Thos F. Anderson   8. James Starrett
   3. Wm Baker   9. Thos Cox
   4. Thos Carnes   10. Allen Chandler
   5. John Smith   11. George King
   6. William Glover   12. James Mitchell

John Neal   }
 vs   } Trespass on the case
Christopher Denman }

Jury N° 1

We, the Jurors, find for the plaintiffs $100.00, with Cost of Suit.

                 Jo^s Reed, foreman

John Tabor, indorsee } of
Aquilla Shockley }
    vs   } Debt
Andrew Tate &   }   Van
davis   }

Jury Nº 1

We, the Jury, find for the plaintiff the Sum of forty five dollars, with interest & Cost of Suit.

                                        Joˢ Reed, foreman

William Bush, Indorsee }
    vs   } Case
Francis Williams   }

Settled at the Deft's Cost.

October Term 1815

Edmund King &   }
William Bush, trading } under
the name of }
King & Bush   }
    vs   } Case
Lewis Williams   }

I confess Judgment to the plaintiffs for the Sum of forty three dollars six and a quarter Cents, with interest and Cost of Suit.

5ᵗʰ Decʳ 1815   Lewis Williams

John Doe, Ex dem } Newal
Walton, Senʳ }
    vs   } Ejectment
Richard Roe   }
James Langston } &
others   }

Jury Nº 1 we find for the Defendants, with

cost of suit.

                                        Joˢ Reed, foreman

John Tabor, Guardian } of
Thomas Gorham }
    vs   } Debt
Christopher Baker }
Surviving obligor }

I do hereby confess Judgment in favour of the plaintiff for the Sum of one hundred dollars, with interest & Cost of Suit.

5th Decr 1815   Jeptha V. Harris, Defts Atty

Woodson Roberts, for   } the
use of David Bollenger }
    vs   } Debt
Christopher Baker }
Surviving Obligor }

I do hereby confess Judgment in favour of the plaintiff for the Sum of forty eight dollars, with interest & Cost of Suit.

5th Decr 1815   Jeptha V. Harris, Deft Atty

———

October Term 1815

Thomas Clark }
    vs   } Trover & Conversion
Joseph Cook, Esqr }

Settled at plaintiff Cost.

Georgia, Franklin Superior C. Oct. Term 1815

John Tabor, guardian } of
Thos Gorham }
vs   } Christopher
Baker }
Surviving obligor }

&

Woodson Roberts, for }
the use of David Ballenger
}   vs   }
Christopher Baker }
Surviving obligor }

On two obligations, one Dated the 28th Day of December 1810, Given for the Sum of Sixty Six dollars & fifty Cents with one [faint] Cent on said obligation for twelve dollars & fifty Cents, in which Eli Bryan was principal & the Said Baker Security, made payable twelve months after date to the Said John Tabor, Guardian as aforesaid. The other dated the 17 day of May 1811, & made payable to Woodson Roberts, Guardian of Becca Stevenson, three days after date for the Sum of One hundred dollars, in which the Said Eli Bryan is principal & Christopher Baker Security. Judgment against Christopher Baker in both the above mentioned Cases. On motion, it is ordered, that the Clerk of this Court deliver to Christopher Baker, or his attorney, the said obligations that he may have his remedy against the Representatives of the principal obligor, Eli Bryan. In retaining a true Copy of the said obligations in office.

John Brice, assignee }
   vs } Debt Bail Samuel Tate
}

Jury N° 1

We, the Jurors, find for the plaintiff five hundred Dollars, with interest & Cost of Suit.

            Jo^s Reed, foreman

The State   }
vs } Ind^t Enveigling negro George Troman }

True Bill.   John R. Brown, foremen

The State   }
  vs   } Indict Enveigling &C
Robert Fullerton }

No Bill.   John R. Brown, Foreman

The State   } vs
} Ind^t murder
Robert Fullerton }

No Bill.   John R. Brown, Foreman William Boling }
  vs   } Case
Joseph Hamilton & }
Margaret Turk }

Jury N° 2 we, the Jury, find for the plaintiff sixty dollars, with interest and Cost of Suit.

 Thomas F. Anderson, foreman of the Jury

William B. Wofford }

vs } Case
Hudson Moss }

we, the Jury, find for the plaintiff one hundred dollars, with interest and Cost of Suit.

Thomas F. Anderson, Foreman of the Jury

October Term 1815

Heirs & Representatives } of
Peter Williamson, }
Respondants }
vs } Bill for Discovery & Distribution
Edmund King & }
Elizabeth King, Exors of }
Peter Williamson, Dec^d }
appellants }

It being Stated to the Court by Complainants' Counsel, that the amount of the Judgment in the above Case, or some part thereof, hath been paid into the Sheriff's hands. On Motion of Counsel. It is ordered, that the Sheriff shew cause at the hour of 9 O'Clock tomorrow morning, or so soon as Counsel can be heard, what amount hath been received by him & why he doth not pay over to the Complainants' Solicitor the amount in his hands.

George W. Moor, for }
the use of Thomas Hyde }
    vs } Case
Martin Boon & } William Legg
}

we, the Jury, find for the plaintiff one hundred and seventy dollars, with interest and Cost of Suit.

Jo^s Reed, foreman

John M. Dooly }
    vs } Case
Garland Lane }

we find for the plaintiff Eighty five Dollars, with Interest and Costs of Suit.

Jo^s Reed, foreman

William Hooper }
    vs } Case
John Hooper }

Jury N° 2

we, the Jury, find for the plaintiff one hundred and fifty Dollars, with interest and Cost of Suit.

    Thomas F. Anderson,   Foreman of the Jury

Asa Leach, for the } use
of Samuel Tate }
 vs   } Debt
Charles Warren }

Jury N° 1 we find for the plaintiff the Sum of fifty five dollars, with Interest and

Cost of Suit.

        Jo^s Reed, foreman

~~Thomas Ivy~~ }
~~vs~~ }
Adam Shuffield }
vs } Franklin Sup^r Court Thomas Ivy }

The parties in this Case mutually agree to Submit all matters in Controversy between them in the above Case to the final arbitrament of Thomas Anderson, Nathaniel Wofford, Bradock Harris, & Berry Page, with power of umprage, whose award when made & signed by them, or a majority of them, if made before the next Term & returned, Shall be Conclusive.

Dudley Jones }
 vs } Case
Reuben Payne }

Jury N° 2 we, the Jury, find for the plaintiff thirty dollars, with interest and

Cost of Suit.

    Thomas F. Anderson,
Foreman of the Jury

Wm B. Wofford }
vs } verdict & Judgment Octr Term 1815 Hudson Moss }

The defendant, Hudson Moss, being dissatisfied with the verdict in the above case, came into ~~office~~ Court with Caleb Griffith, his security, and paid the cost, and prayed an appeal, and him and his security acknowledged themselves bound to the plaintiff for the eventual Condemnation money & Cost. Given under our hands & seals this 5th day of December 1815.

Test. Maxfield H. Payne, Clk   Hudson Moss, Caleb Griffith

John Nail }
    vs   } Verdict & Judgment Octr Term 1815
Christopher Denman }

The defendant, Christopher Denman, being dissatisfied with the verdict in the above case, came into Court with [blank], his security, and paid the Cost, and prayed an appeal, and him & his security acknowledged themselves bound to the plaintiff for the eventual condemnation money & Cost. Given under our hands & Seals this 5th day of December 1815.
Test. [blank]   [blank]

The Court then adjourned untill to morrow morning Nine O'Clock.

Test. Maxfield H. Payne, Clk   Young Gresham

October Term 1815

The Court met according to adjournment Wednesday the 6th of December 1815.

Present, his honor Judge Gresham.

Test. Maxfield H. Payne, Clk

Ex^d ~~Young Gresham~~

The Exors of John Dilbert }
    vs   } Bill in Equity
Robert Cimmons &   }
Eliz Cimmins   }

To perpetuate Testimony, on motion of Sol^r for Complainants, it is ordered, that the defendants plead, answer, or demur, not demurring alone, within three months, or the Bill will be taken pro confesso, and that a Copy of this order be Served on the Defendants, or their Sol^{rs}, within two months of this day, 6th Decr 1815.

Georgia   }
Franklin County   } To his Honor Young Gresham, Judge of the Superior Court of the Western Circuit.

1) The petition of J. W. Campbell Humbly Sheweth to your honor, that for some time past your petitioner has been in the pursuit of Legal information, with a view of becoming a Practitioner, and for this purpose he now makes application to your honor and prays that [smudge] if on examination his proficiency and his acquirements Should be satisfactory, that the benefit of the Statute regulating the admission of

Attorneys may be extended to him.

J. W. Campbell, Pet^r

2) Georgia }
Franklin County } I certify that J. W. Campbell has applied himself to the Study of the Law under my tuition for upwards of eighteen months and that he is twenty one years of age.

4th Nov. 1815   Duncan G. Campbell

3) Georgia }
Franklin County } I have been for a considerable time acquainted with John W. Campbell and his general deportment has been regular, upright, & Exemplary.

4th Nov. 1815   T. H. Harnes

4) Committee appointed, Mr Paine, Mr Ge^o Cook, Collo Harris.

5) Georgia }
Franklin County } We, the Committee who were appointed to examine the Within named applicant, have performed that duty, and are unanimously of opinion that he is qualified for the practice of Law and recommend that he be admitted accordingly.
6th Decr 1815   Ge^o Cook
                                                     Walton Harris
                                                     Edward Paine

6) I, John Warlty Campbell, do Solemnly Swear that I will well and truly demean myself as an attorney, Solicitor, and councellor in the Several Courts of Law and Equity in this State, that I will Support, maintain, and defend the Constitution of this State and the Constitution of the United States.

So help me God.

Sworn to in open Court }   J. W. Campbell
this 6th day of December }
1815   }

Test. Maxfield H. Payne, Clk

Georgia }
Franklin County } Superior Court October Term 1815

7) John W. Campbell, having by the foregoing petition applied for the benefit of the Statute regulating the admission of attornies and having by the report of a Committee appointed for that purpose, passed an approved examination, and the Said John W. Campbell, having this day also appeared in open Court and Submitted himself to a

public examination which is Satisfactory to the Court, and having taken and Subscribed the foregoing Oath.

It is ordered, that the Said John W. Campbell be and he is hereby admitted to the practice of Law in the Several Courts of Law and Equity in this State.

Joseph Ratchford, appl }
     vs   } In Equity
Larkin Cleveland, Ex^{or} }

Superior Court Oct. Term 1815 no parties

On motion of Counsel for respondant, it is ordered, that parties be made at the next Term or the case to be dismissed, unless good cause be Shewn to the Contrary.

The State   }
    vs   } Ind^t assault
John Dobbs   }
Peter Dobbs, J^r }
John Pearson, J^r }

True Bill.   John R. Brown, Foreman

The State   }   vs   }
Ind^t assault
Jeremiah Taylor, J^r }
& Thomas Townsend, J^r }

No Bill.   John R. Brown, Foreman

The State   }   vs
} Ind^t trespass
Adam Shuffield }
No Bill.   John R. Brown, Foreman

The   State
}   vs
}
John Everett }

Joseph Woodall, who was the Security for Everett in this Case, delivered up the said Eveverett into Court, & thereupon was discharged from his recognizance.

The State   }
    vs   } Ind^t Petit Larceny
John English }

True Bill.   John R. Brown, Foreman

The State   }
     vs   } Ind^t Assault
Benjamin Starrett }

                                              John R. Brown, foreman
True Bill.

The State   }
      vs   } Ind^t Petit
Larceny Daniel Blagg } Jury N° 1, Viz.

    1. Absalom Baker   7. John Campbell
    2. Frederick Braszell   8. Owen Andrews
    3. Obediah Ayers   9. Joseph Reed
    4. John Baker   10. James Jones
    5. John Dorsey   11. Wm Blackwell
    6. Wm Holbrook   12. Thos Clark

we, the Jurors, find the prisoner at the Barr guilty.

                                              Jo^s Reed, foreman

The State } vs } Indict Petit Larceny
Israel Blag } Verdict Guilty

Sentence of the Court

You, Israel Blag, are to be taken immediately from this Bar to the public whipping post in the town of Carnesville & there to receive on Your bare back by the proper officer fifteen lashes with a whip or cow Skin & be thence discharged on the payment of Cost.

                 Franklin Superior Court Oct Term 1815

(Copy)

Due Dooly & Carter the Sum of Sixty dollars and thirty two Cents for value received this 1st July 1809.

                                Elisha Wilkinson

Credit in 1812 for $34.62½.   Dooly & Carter, Jarrat Carter
Georgia   }
Franklin County } This day personally came and appeared before me John Cleveland, who being duly Sworn, Saith that the following is a true Copy, to the best of his recollection, a note or due bill given by Elisha Wilkinson To Dooly & Carter, and by them indorsed to Jarrat Carter, the Same who indorsed it to your deponant for a

Valuable consideration, and that the said original was lost by this deponant on the 4th July last, and it is so lost or mislaid, that he cannot find it. Sworn to & Subscribed before me this 6th Oct[r] 1815.

James Mitchell, J. P.   John Cleveland

Georgia   }
Franklin County } To the hon[ble] Superior Court now Sitting

The petition ___

of John Cleveland humbly prays that the foregoing Copy of a note may be established in lieu of the Original, as the original is lost, in terms of the law in Such case made and provided. 6th December 1815

                                       John Cleveland

Franklin Superior Court Oct Term 1815

On motion of J. Smith, Counsel for John Cleveland, Stating that a due Bill, of which he has filed a true Copy in this Court, is lost and it is not in his power to procure it.

It is therefore Ordered, that the said Copy be Established in lieu of the original, according to the Statute in Such Case made, unless good cause be Shewn to the contrary, provided that a copy of this rule be published in some public Gazette of this State for the Space of Six months previous to the next Term of this Court.

The Court then adjourned untill to morrow morning Nine O'Clock.

Ex[d]   Young Gresham

The Court met according to adjournment the 7th day of December 1815. Present, his Honor Judge Gresham.

Test.   Gresham

Maxfield H. Payne, Clk

———

Grand Jurors drawn for April Term 1816.

1. Neely Dobson
2. James H. Little
3. Joel Strange
4. Nathan[l] Wofford
5. Tho[s] Anderson
6. John Wryly
7. Robert Bruce
8. Cabot Griffin

19. Robert Hacket
20. John Allen, J[r]
21. Richard Say
22. Benj[n] Love
23. Garrett L. Sandidge
24. John Hudson
25. Lowry Gillaspie
26. David Payne

9. Joseph Chandler, B. C.
10. Richd Hooper
11. John Martin[?]
12. Freeman Hardy
13. Edward D. Carrell
14. Hugh B. Greenwood
15. John Mayfield, J^r
16. Joseph Martin
17. Dudly Jones
18. Joseph Payne

27. Hugh Davidson
28. Redfern Weems
29. Timothy Terrell
30. John Duncan, J^r
31. Richd Hutcherson
32. Moses Guest, Esqr
33. Saml H. Everett
34. Wm Hulsey
35. John Bush
36. Joseph Morris

Pettit Jurors for April Term 1816

1. James Hargrove, J^r
2. George Carpenter
3. Thos Clark, J^r
4. Robert Williams
5. Joseph Edward
6. Benjn Tucker
7. Saml Prenett

8. Wm Smith, B. B.
9. Tignal Jones
10. Jesse Blackwell
11. Thos Balwin
12. Wm Goodson
13. John Garrisson
14. John Barton

15. Isaac Allbritton
16. John Harber
17. Asa Leach
18. Wm Gober, M. C.
19. Thos Morgan
20. Michael Ragsdale
21. Wm Wilson
22. John Odam
23. George Longmire
24. Thos Carter
25. Jonathan Bangs
26. Nathl Williams
27. George Tilman
28. John Clarkson
29. Robt Bond
30. Wm Jones

31. Mathew McCarter
32. Edwd Isham
33. Robt Harrison
34. Moses Sanders, J^r
35. Wyatt Cleveland
36. Elisha Cook
37. Wm Holland
38. James Wofford
39. Hez^k Stephens
40. John Bellamy
41. Major Neal
42. Clem^t Carrell
43. Ja^s W^{m}son
44. Peter Brown
45. Joel Lausone
46. Richd Bond, J^r
47. John C. Watters
48. John Bargey

Thomas Lenoir, Adm^r } of Mary Lenoir }
    vs   } In Equity for Distribution, &C
James Hollingsworth, Adm^r } of Saml Hollingsworth, dec^d }

On motion of Sol{r} for Complainant, it is ordered, that the Defendant plead, answer, or demure, not demurring alone, on or before the first day of next term, or the said Bill will be taken pro Confesso.

Beck & Pope, for the } use
of John Beck }
    vs } Case
Benjamin King }

Dismissed.

———

Stephen Dixon, appl }
    vs } Ejectment
Jesse Holbrook & }
others, Resp{ts} }

Jury Sworn
    1. Thompson Moore   7. Edmund Henly
    2. Robt Neal   8. Edmund King, Jn{r}
    3. John Nail   9. Isaac J. Barratt
    4. James Ramsey   10. Meredith Brown
    5. James Martin   11. Richard Gray
    6. Thomas Hollingsworth   12. William Bush

the above Jury discharged from the Consideration of the Case.

The State } vs } Ind{t} Grand Larceny
Absalom Cornelius }

True Bill.   John R. Brown, foreman

George Watkins }   vs }
Bill & Injunction
John Hooper }
Robert Hackett & }
William Cleveland }

On motion of Sol{r} for Comp{ts}, it is ordered, that the defendants plead, answer, or demur, not demurring alone, by the first day of the next Term, or the said Bill will be taken pro Confesso.

Heirs of ~~Jacob~~ Saml Hollingsworth, decd, writ of partition Received in open Court & admitted & ordered to be Recorded.

———

Heirs of Peter Williamson }
    vs } In Equity Fi Fa
Edmund King & }

Elizabeth King   }

Rule on the Sheriff to Shew Cause why the money in his hands collected on the above case Should Not be paid to the Complainants' Solicitor, after hearing the parties. It is ordered that the Sheriff do forthwith pay Over to Thos P. Carnes, Solicitor for Complainants, all the money in his hands Collected on the above fi fa, except one twelfth part, to which Edmund King, in right of his wife, is entitled.

On motion October Term 1815

It is ordered, that the calling of the appearance Docket be dispensed with at the present Term & no exceptions at the next Term, as to matter of form to operate as a Nonsuit.

Copy filed.

Due Dooly & Carter the sum of sixty dollars and thirty two Cents for Value Received this 1st July 1809.

Elisha Wilkinson

Credit on this note for $34.62½ this [blank] day of 1812.

We indorse the within note to Jarratt Carter for Value Received.

Dooly & Carter

Oct. Term 1815

Georgia } Franklin County }
Rule Nisi

William Davis, having filed a Bill praying for a Divorce, returnable to this Court, against Nancy, his wife, and the officer having returned not to be found, and it being Suggested to the Court that the said Nancy resides out of the County. On motion of Green W. Smith, Solicitor for William Davis, it is ordered, that the said Nancy in person, or by her attorney, be and appear before the honorable the Superior Court, to be held in & for said County on the Second Monday in April next, then & there to make her defence, Otherwise the Court will proceed thereon as to Justice Shall appertain, & that a copy of this rule be published in one of the Gazettes of this State once a month for four months.

In indorse the within note to John Cleveland for Value received.

Jarratt Carter

October Term 1815

And now at this Term, comes the plaintiff into Court by Green W. Smith, his attorney, and excepts to the Sufficiency of the bail taken in this case, viz. Adam Shuffield, who has been taken as special Bail for the defendant in this Case by the Clerk, because he is not solvent & unable to pay the amount Claimed by the plaintiff in this Case, he therefore prays that the Clerk Shew Cause at the next Term why he Should not be held as Special Bail in this Case according to law. 8th Decr 1815

Green W. Smith, Plffs attorney

We, the Grand Jury for the County of Franklin, at October Term 1815, Congratulate our fellow Citizens on the return of peace, its concomitant advantages, we are also happy to State that the internal affairs of our Country require no interference of this

body.

We also present our thanks to his honor, Judge Gresham, for his unremitting attention during the present term.

John R. Brown

The Court then adjourned untill Court in Course.

Test. M. H. Payne, Clk

Exd   Young Gresham

April Term 1816

The Superior Court of Franklin County met on the Eight day, being the Second monday in April 1816. Present, His Honor Judge Gresham.

According to the Exigance of a Writ of Venire to him directed, the high Sheriff of said County returned Said Writ into Court, with the following persons Summoned & Sworn as Grand Jurors.

1. James H. Little
2. Neely Dobson
3. Nathl Wofford
4. Thos Anderson
5. Robert Bruce
6. Joseph Chandler
7. John McEntire
8. Hugh B. Greenwood
9. Jos Martin
13. G. L. Sandridge
14. Lowry Gillaspie
15. Redfearn Weems
16. John Duncan
17. Moses Guest
18. John Bush
19. Joseph Morris
20. Joshua Hudson
21. David Payne

10. Edward Carrell   22. Benjn Love

11. Joseph Payne   23. Richd Hooper

12. Richard Say

John Bowman   }   <u>April Term 1816</u>
   vs   } Libel for Divorce
Winnifred Bowman }

Jury Sworn.

1. Thos Anderson   7. G. L. Sandige
2. Robert Bruce   8. Lowry Gillaspie
3. Hugh B. Greenwood   9. John Duncan
4. Joseph Martin   10. Moses Guest
5. Joseph Payne   11. John Bush
6. Richard Say   12. Joseph Morris

We find the Sufficient proofs have been referred to our Consideration to authorize a total divorce, that is to say, a divorce a vincula matrimonie upon legal principles between the parties in this case.

                                 Joseph Morris, Foreman

Pettit Jury N° 1

1. Thos Clark   7. John Harber
2. Samuel Prewitt   8. Asa Leach
3. Tignal Jones   9. John Clarkson
4. Jesse Blackwell   10. Wm Gober
5. Thos Baldwin   11. Thos Morgan
6. John Barton   12. Wm Wilson

Pettit Jury N° 2

1. George Longmires   7. Hezekiah Stephens
2. Thos Carter   8. John Bellamy
3. Joseph Edwards   9. Major Neal
4. Mathew McCarter   10. Clement Carrell
5. Moses Sanders   11. James Williamson
6. Elisha Cook   12. Peters Brown

John Cowden   }
   vs   }

Temple Carpenter }

Settled at Defendant's Cost.

Benjn Perry }
vs }
Absalom Cleveland } Settled

& Cost Paid.

John R. Brown }
   vs } Case
Boley Conner, adm{r} }

Jury N° 1

We, the Jury, find for the plaintiff the Sum of seventy three dollars & Eighty one Cents, with Cost of Suit.

                              Wm Gober, Fm

William Tate }
   vs } Debt
Francis Callaway }

Settled at Defendant's Cost.

John F. Barnett }
   vs } Case
Jonathan Baugh }

Jury N° 1

We find for plaintiff thirty seven dollars and fifty cents, with interest & costs.

                              Wm Gober, Fm

———

Sterling Harris }
   vs } Certiorari
James Haley }
Settled.

The Court then adjourned untill to morrow morning Nine O'Clock.

Test. Maxfield H. Payne, Clk

Ex{d}   Young Gresham

The Court met According to adjournment tuesday the 9th April 1816. Present, his Honor Judge Gresham.

Jury N° 1

1. Thos Clark
2. Saml Prewitt
3. Tignal Jones
4. Jesse Blackwell
5. Thos Baldwin
6. John Barton
7. Mathew McCarter
8. Asa Leach
9. John Clarkson
10. Wm Gober
11. Thos Morgan
12. Wm Wilson

George Turman } vs } Trover & Conversion
Nimrod Leathers & his wife }
Nancy Leathers, formerly }
Nancy Reynolds }

Jury N° 1

We, the Jury, find for the plaintiff four thousand dollars, which may be discharged by delivering the negroes & other property mentioned in the declaration to the plaintiff, or his attorney, within ten days, & Costs of Suit.

Wm Gober, Fm

The Executors of John Gilbert }
    vs } Bill in Equity to perfuate Testamony &C
Robert Cimmins & }
Elizabeth Cimmins }

The defendants having been ordered, by rule obtained at the last term, to plead, answer, or demur, not demurring alone, within three months, which rule was duly Served upon the Defts' Solicitor. And the Said defendants having failed to comply with the Rule aforesaid, it is ordered, considered, & deemed by the Court, that the Said Bill be taken pro confesso. and that the Testimony of the following Witnesses (heretofore taken by way of commission filed in the Clerk's office of this Court, a transcript of which testimony is also annexed to said Bill) to wit, Isaac Friar, Aquilla Byford, Edward Riley, Labon Holland, Adam Moore, Janus Coats, William Maxwell, John Cunningham, William Loley, Peter Smith, William Moore, James Holland, Sarah Holland, be perpetuated, to serve in perpetuam rei memoriam of the title of the Complainants, Executors of the Said John Gilbert, dec^d, of, in, and to the negro Slaves (and their increase) in the said Bill mentioned, and that the said Testimony be recorded.

John R. Brown }
    vs } Verdict

Boley Conner, adm^r } of
Eli Bryan, dec^d }

And now Comes the defendant, Boley Conner, administrator of s^d Eli Bryan, dec^d, and being dissatisfied with the verdict in the above case, paid up the Cost and prays an appeal. 9th April 1816
appeal granted   }

Test.   }   Boley Conner, Adm^r of
Maxfield H. Payne, Clk }   Eli Bryan, Deceas^d

The Court then adjourned untill to morrow Morning Nine O'Clock.

Test. Maxfield H. Payne, Clk

Ex^d Young Gresham

The Court according to adjournment Wednesday the 10th April 1816. Present, his Honor Judge Gresham.

Boley Conner, Adm^{rs} of }
Eli Bryan   } vs } Covenant
Edward Bryan   }

Jury N° 1

We find for the plaintiff One thousand dollars, to be discharged titles, according to the condition of the Bond due and on to the said plaintiff within thirty days, with Costs.

Wm Gober, fm

Wood & Kilpatrick }
     vs   } Case
Robert Harrisson }
Settl^d & Cost paid.

Adam Shuffield }
 vs } Case Thom Jay }

William Russell }
     vs   } Debt
Bryan Ward   }
James R. Wyly }
& John Lane   }

Jury Nº 1

We, the Jury, find for the plaintiff the Sum of four hundred and twenty four dollars, with interest and Cost of Suit.

           Wm Gober, fm

Wm Crenshaw }
  vs   } Attachment returnable to Franklin Sup^r Court Oct. Term 1816
John W. Cloud & } Adam
Cloud }

On motion of J. Smith, counsel for plaintiff, Stating that the attachment in the above Case is levied on a negro man named David as the property of the defendants & is now confined in the common Jail of this County, by which a considerable expense will be incurred to the parties in this case previous to the trial of this Case. it is therefore ordered, that the Sheriff advertise said negro for Sale & after giving legal notice, Sell him & place the amount in the Clerk's office of this Court, Subject to the further order of this Court.

[In the left margin of the page, the clerk wrote the following.]

This order set order by order of Court.

―――

William Davis }
  vs   } Libel for a Divorce
Nancy Davis }

Special Jury Sworn.
   1. Neely Dobson   7. H. B. Greenwood
   2. Nathl Wofford   8. Jo^s Martin
   3. Thos Anderson   9. Edward Carrell
   4. Robert Bruce   10. Joseph Payne
   5. Joseph Chandler   11. Richd Say
   6. John McIntire   12. G. L. Sandrige

We find that Sufficient proofs have been referred to our consideration to authorize a total divorce, that is to say, a divorce a vincula matrimonie upon legal principles between the parties in this Case.

           John McIntire, foreman

The State }
  vs   } Verdict & Sentence man Slaughter at Superior Court Joseph
Edwards } Franklin April Term 1815

On Motion of Counsel for the said Joseph Edwards, stating that he has before this Court a full pardon from the Executive of this State, he therefore prays to be hence discharged. It is therefore ordered, that the said Joseph Edwards be discharged from said Conviction & said pardon be entered On Record.

State of Georgia

By his Excellency Peter Early, Governor and Commander in Chief of the Army and Navy of this State and the Militia thereof.

To all and Singular, the Judges, Sheriffs, Jailors, Constables, and other Ministers of Justice, to Whom these presents Shall Come, or whom the same may Concern, Greetings.

Whereas, at a Superior Court held in and for the County of Franklin at April Term Eighteen Hundred and fifteen before the Honorable Young Gresham, one of the Judges of the Superior Courts of this State, a Certain Joseph Edwards was Indicted for the Murder of Joseph Cook, of said County, and was Convicted of Manslaughter, upon which the Court pronounced the following Sentence, to wit. It is ordered by the Court, that Joseph Edwards appear on Wednesday of the next Term of this Court between the Hours of ten O'clock in the forenoon and two O'clock in the afternoon of that day, and then at this Barr of this Court you are to be branded on the brawn of the left thumb with a hot Iron by the proper Officer with the Letter M, and then to be discharged On the payment of Cost, in the meantime you are to give Ample security on the Penalty of five Thousand dollars for your Appearance at the day above mentioned to receive the sentence of the Court here pronounced as will more fully and at large appear by reference to the record of proceedings of said Court.

And, whereas, a petition hath been presented to the Executive, Signed by a Number of Citizens .

of said County of Franklin, praying for reasons therein set forth that pardon may be granted

[In the left margin of the page, the clerk wrote the following.]

Peter Early {Seal}

---

to the said Joseph Edwards, and from a statement of the evidence given in on the trial which has been furnished by the Judge presiding. it appearing that the Case is One in titled to executive clemency, I have thought proper to pardon and do by virtue of the power and Authority in me vested by the seventh section of the second article of the Constitution of this State, Pardon the aforesaid Joseph Edwards for the Crime of which he has been convicted as aforesaid. And, he is hereby exonerated and discharged from the effects of the same, so far as relates to his being branded on the brawn of the left thumb with a hot Iron by proper officer with the letter M, but nothing herein contained shall be so [blot] Construed as to exonerate him, the said Joseph Edwards, from the Payment of Cost.

Given under my hand and the Seal of the Executive at the State House in Milledgeville this twenty fifth day of April in the year of our Lord One Thousand eight hundred and fifteen and in the Thirty Ninth year of the Independence of the United States of America. By the Governor, Edward Early, Sectrey.

The State }
    vs   } Franklin Superior Court
Wm O. Whitney } Sci fa on forfeiture of Recognizance

On motion of the Solicitor General, Shewing an Act of the General Assembly of this State passed at November Session eighteen hundred & fifteen requiring him to enter Satisfaction upon the Recognizance forfeited in this Case of record & to deliver up

---

the Said Recognizance to the said Whitney & Payne upon the payment of Costs & as [blank] to enter Such Satisfaction.

Ordered, that satisfaction be entered upon the Said Recognizance of record, & the costs being first paid. It is hereby further ordered, that the said bond be & is hereby declared to be Satisfied, & that the Same be delivered to the said Wm O. Whitney & Nathaniel

Payne.

The State   }   vs
} Ind^t Pujery
Peter Waggoner }

Jury N° 1

We, the Jurors, find the prisoner at the bar guilty.

                                              Wm Gober, fm

Thomas Coker   }
    vs   } Trover & Conversion
Starling Strange }

Nonsuit.
Kinneth Findley }
    vs   } Debt
Robert Bruce   }

I confess Judgment to the plaintiff One hundred & twenty dollars, with interest & Cost of Suit.

                                      Jeptha V. Harris, Defts Atty

Pettit Jury N° 2

1. George Longmires	7. John Bellamy
2. Thoˢ Carter	8. Clement Carrell
3. Joseph Edwards	9. James Williamson
4. Moses Sanders	10. ~~John Harber~~ Wᵐ Scott
5. Elisha Cook	11. Elias Burges
6. Hezekiah Stephens	12. Nathˡ Williams

The State }
    vs } Indᵗ misdemeanor
Geº Turman }

True Bill.   Jaˢ H. Little, Foreman

George Turman }
    vs   } Trover & Conversion
Nancy Reynolds }

Peter Dobbs & Jeremiah Dobbs, who were securities for the Defendant in the above Case, Came into Court & delivered up the Defendant, & thereupon was discharge.

The State }
vs } Indᵗ Larceny from the person Elias Wood }

True Bill.   James H. Little, Foreman

The Court then adjourned untill to morrow morning Nine O'Clock.

Test. Maxfield H. Payne, Clk

Exᵈ   Young Gresham

George Turman   }
    vs   } Trover & verdict for plff
<u>Nancy Reynolds</u>   }
& Nimrod Leathers's }
intermarriage with   }
Deft suggested at }
April Term 1816   }

And now Comes Nimrod Leathers, who intermarried with Nancy Reynolds, the defendant in this case, into office, and being dissatisfied with the verdict in the above case, has paid up the Cost and prayed an appeal, and at the same time Benjamin Cleveland and Joseph Martin came with him, and as securities, they all Jointly & severally acknowledged bound unto the plaintiff, George Turman, for the final Condemnation money and Costs. As witness our hands & seals This 10ᵗʰ April 1816.
this bond taken & }   Nimrod Leathers
acknowledged   }   Benjᵃ Cleveland

before me & } Joseph Martin
Appeal granted }
Test. Maxfield H. Payne, Clk

The Court met according to adjournment on thursday the 11th April 1816. Present, his honor Judge Gresham.

The State }
vs } Ind[t] Larceny from the person Elias
Wood } Jury Sworn.

    1. Thomas Clark   7. Isaac J. Barrett
    2. Thomas Baldwin   8. John R. Brown
    3. Asa Leach   9. W[m] Brown
    4. Thomas Morgan   10. Absalom Trantham
    5. Joseph Edwards   11. Henry Smith
    6. Elisha Cook   12. John Smith

We, the Jurors, find the prisoner Guilty of Compound larceny, as contained in the first count in this bill of Indictment.

                John R. Brown, foreman

Thomas Ivy, assignee } of
Martin Williams }
   vs   } Case &C
Robert Melton }

Settled at Plaintiff's Cost.

William A. Blackburn }
   vs   } Slander
Joseph Watters }
Settled at Plaintiff's Cost.

Pettit Jury N° 2
    1. George Longmires   7. Nath[l] Williams
    2. Tho[s] Carter   8. Sam[l] Prewett
    3. Moses Sanders   9. Tignal Jones
    4. Hezekiah Stephens 10. Jesse Blackwell
    5. John Bellamy   11. John Burton
    6. Clemment Carrell   12. Mathew McCarter

The State }
    vs } Ind[t]
Assa
James Smith }

True Bill.   James H. Little, foreman
Kinneth Findley }
    vs   } Case
Robert Bruce   }

Jury N° 2

We, the Jury, find for the plaintiff seventeen dollars & twenty five Cents, with Cost.

                                  Jesse Blackwell, Fm

Edmund King, Jn^r }
    vs   } Case
Robert Melton   }

Jury N° 2

We, the Jury, find for the plaintiff the Sum of Sixty five dollars, with interest & Cost of Suit.

                                  Jesse Blackwell, Fm

Jesse Dobbs, assignee } of
Sterling Strange   }
    vs   } Case
Nathaniel Wade   }

I confess Judgment to the plaintiff for two hundred and Seventy two dollars sixty three Cents, with interest & Cost.

                                  A. Lawhon, Deft's Atty

The Court the adjourned till tomorrow morning 9 O'Clock.
Test. Maxfield H. Payne, Clk

Ex^d Young Gresham

The Court according to adjournment on Friday the 12th April 1816. Present, his honor Judge Gresham.

The State   }
    vs   } Indictment for perjury
Peter Wagnon } April Term 1816 Verdict Guilty

It is ordered by the Court, that you, Peter Wagnon, to be taken from this Bar to the common Jail, there to be confined for the Space of thirty days, you are then to pay into the Clerk's Office of this Court fifty dollars, & never more to be capable of bearing

testimony.

The State } vs
} Franklin Super Court Elias Wood
} April Term 1816

Indictment for Compound Larceny, Verdict of Guilty, Sentence

It is ordered by by the Court, that You, Elias Wood, be taken from this Bar to the Common Jail of this County, there to remain in Close Confinement, untill Friday the tenth day of May next, & on that day between the hours of ten O'Clock in the forenoon and three O'Clock in the afternoon, you are to be taken by the proper Officer to a Gallows to be erected in or near the Village of Carnesville, & there to be hung by the neck until you are dead, & may the God of Heaven have mercy on your Soul.

Wm Crenshaw }
    vs   } Attachment
Jno W. Cloud & }
Adam Cloud }

Levied upon a Negroe. & on order, obtained for the Sale of Said Negroe. On motion, it is ruled that the above rented order be Set aside.

Stephen Dixon, appellant }
    vs   } Ejectment
Thomas White & others } Respondants
}

Jury Sworn

1. Nathl Wofford
2. Thos Anderson
3. Robert Bruce
4. Joseph Chandler
5. John McIntire
6. Joseph Martin
7. Edward Carrell
8. Richd Say
9. Garrett L. Sandrige
10. Redfern Weems
11. John Duncan
12. John Bush

We, the Jury, find for the appellant the premises in disputes, with Cost of Suit.

                        Garrett L. Sandridge, F. m.

Henry & Jacob J. Hollingsworth } by their
Next friend & Guardian }
Thomas Lenoir   }
    vs   } Bill for amount, distribution,
Jacob Hollingsworth, Adm^r on the } & Relief Estate of
Samuel Hollingsworth, Dec^d }

Dismissed.

The Court the adjourned till to morrow morning 8 O'Clock.

Test. Maxfield H. Payne, Clk

Ex^d Young Gresham

___

The Court met according to adjournment on Saturday the 13th April 1816. Present, His Honor Judge Gresham.

George Prickett, in right of } his wife Patsey Prickett, } Patsey Taylor, one of the } heirs & legatees of } Charles Taylor, Dec^d }
vs } Franklin Superior Court
George C. Taylor, Ann Taylor,   } April Term 1816
& Elizabeth Taylor, heirs &   } legatees
of said Charles Taylor, Dec^d }

This case, coming on to be heard before the Court, on the Grounds stated in the Caveat.

It is determined, that the Grounds are in Sufficient to Set aside the will or revoke the letters of Executorship Granted by the Court of ordinary, whereupon, it is ordered, that the will be established in its Original Shop. That is, the words. "their increase be to have it & go to & br Equally divided between the Survivors," which appear Obliterated & erased in the will, be reinstated, & the words interlined, to wit, "Will be given to my son Ge^o C. Taylor," be erased & obliterated.

___

Grand Jurors Drawn for Octr Term 1816
1. James Tate   19. Wm Thomas
2. John Wormack   20. Wm Hackett, Esq
3. Reuben Shotwell   21. Joseph Terrell
4. John Mullin   22. Thos Mayfield
5. Wm Ward   23. Richd Gray, Esq
6. Sampson Lane   24. Joseph Chandler, G. C.
7. Boley Conner   25. Benjn Cleveland, S. C.
8. Sterling Chandler 26. Devroux Jarrett
9. Joseph Reed, Esq 27. James Allan, Esq
10. Dudley Jones   28. Fred^k Beall
11. Charles Sesser   29. Saml Haden
12. Wyatt Cleveland 30. Joseph Walters, Esq
13. Asa Allen   31. Edm^d King, J^r
14. John E. Carson   32. Elias Burges
15. Anthony Story   33. James Mitchell, Esq
16. Robert Barns   34. Henry Smith
17. Foweler F. Adrine   35. Simon Terrell
18. Wm Pool   36. Richd Allen

Pettit Jurors Drawn for Oct[r] 1816

1. Greenberry Jewell
2. James McClain
3. Fred[k] Holley
4. Harris Branch
5. Michael Box, Se[r]
6. Reuben Baxter
7. Sam[l] Burton
8. Benj[n] Slater
9. W[m] Tucker
10. Tho[s] Davis, J[r]
11. Lemberd King
12. Sam[l] Dailey

---

13. Pleasant Holley
14. Benj[n] Wofford
15. W[m] Eddins
16. Aaron Robert
17. Darias Echols
18. Nathan Petitford
19. James Reed, J[r]
20. John Conner
21. Ephram Malry
22. John Anthony
23. Levy Garrisson
24. Christopher Garrison
25. James Jordan
26. Chafin Chatham
27. Gabriel Smith
28. Charles Cawthen
29. W[m] Lowry
30. Peter Corkerham
31. Rich[d] Hardon
32. John Carrell
33. Wyly Hogwood
34. Charles Baker
35. John Holcom
36. George Gober
37. W[m] Westbrook
38. Nicholas Sewell
39. James Haley
40. Elias Jordan
41. Calob Garrisson
42. Sam[l] Morgan
43. Rob[t] Saxon
44. Tho[s] Maxwell
45. John Bowman
46. Tho[s] Nunn
47. Isaac Love
48. Tho[s] Jones

Franklin Superior Court April Term 1816
We, the Grand Jury for the body of the County of Franklin, taking into view the present flourishing Situation of our Country, are impressed with the duty of expressing the pleasing sensations we feel upon a subject so gratifying. While the motto of Freedom & liberty is subjoined to that of peace and plenty, we discover from the Scarcity of bills of indictment brought before us at this term, that unanimity, honesty, & friendship appear to pervade the Citizens of our County. These are Considerations truly gratifying & call for ___

congratulations and high expressions of approbation towards our fellow Citizens. It has been with a dignee of pleasure that we have witnessed in his honor Judge Gresham a firmness & integrity suitable to his dignified station. We therefore hope that we shall not be Considered as merely formal an insincere in tendering to him our hearty thanks for his assiduous attention to the business of the Court during the present Term. We request that these our presentments be published in one of the public gazettes of this State.

James H. Little, fm   Joseph Payne
Robert Bruce   Benjamin Love
Edward Carrell   John Duncan

        Joshua Hudson   Joseph Martin
        John McEntire   Moses Guest, J^r
        Richard Hooper   Joseph Chandler
        Redfearn Weems   Lowry Gillaspie
        Richd Say   Thomas Anderson
        Joseph Morris   John Bush
        Hugh B. Greenwood   Garrett L. Sandige

The Court ordered the presentments to be published in the Georgia Journal.

Daniel Beall   } Amos
Bratcher   }
   vs   } Trover
John Westbrook }

Verdict for plff on the appeal. Rule Nisi for a New Trial. It is agreed by Counsil, that the Grounds for a new Trial be argued at Wilks Sup^r Court in June next, it is further agreed that if the Court Should be of Opinion that there Shall be a new trial, that the next Term ___

of this Court shall be considered as the first trial Term, and it is also agreed that if the Court discharges the Rule, that the Execution may issue immediately thereafter.

The Same } vs } Trover
Stephen Westbrook }

Verdict for Deft, Rule for New Trial
It is agreed that the said Rule be argued at the next Term of Wiks Court and also that the next Term of this Court shall be Considered as the first trial Term in the event of a New trial being ordered.

Georgia } Franklin County } April Term 1816
Rule Nisi

Polley Hamilton, having filed a Lible praying for a Divorce, returnable to this Court, against Joseph Hamilton, her husband, & the said Lible being returned by the Sheriff of said County, non est inventus, and it being Suggested to the Court that the said Joseph resides out of the Jurisdictional limits of this State. On motion of Green W. Smith, Solicitor for the said Polley Hamilton, It is ordered, that the said Joseph be and appear in person, or by attorney, at the Superior Court to be held in and for said County upon the Second monday in October next, then and there to make his defence, if any he has, Otherwise the Court will proceed thereon as to Justice Shall appertain, & that a Copy

of this Rule be Served on the defendant or published in One of the Gazettes of this State Once a month for four months previous thereto.

John Tate   }
  vs   } Certiorari

John Sutton } proceedings from the Justices Court set aside.

James Logan } vs
} Certiorari
Absalom Holcom & }
Timothy Terrell }

Certiorari Sustained & proceedings below Set aside on the Grounds that the assumption was by one person for another & not reduced to writing.

Walton Harris }
    vs } Certiorari
Arthur Alexander }

Verdict of the Jury below Set aside & a new trial ordered.

John Hooper }
    vs } Trover
Adam Cloud }

Settled & Cost paid.

Stephen Dye }
    vs } Trespass
Benjamin Starrett }
James Mareen }
Settled.

Stephen Dye } vs
} Trespass
Benjamin Starrett }
John E. Carson & }
Thompson Epperson }

Settled.

———

The Court then adjourned till Court in Course.

Thomas Lenorir, adm^r of }
Mary Lenorir }
    vs } In Equity for Distribution
Jacob Hollingsworth, adm^r } of
Saml Hollingsworth, dec^d }

Settled.

Charles L. Mathews }
vs } Fi Fa
Lewis Moulder }

Same } vs }
Fi Fa Same }

Ordered, that the Sheriff pay over the amount of the money raised in the above Cases to the executions in favour F. Beall & filed by him after deducting his Cost.

The Court then adjourned till Court in Course.

Test. Maxfield H. Payne, Clk

Ex[d] Young Gresham

October Term 1816

The Superior Court of Franklin County met on the fourteenth day, being the Second Monday in October 1816. Present, His Honor Judge Gresham.

According to the Exigence of a Writ of Venire to him directed, the high Sheriff of Said County returned Said Writ into Court, with the following persons Summoned & Sworn as Grand Jurors, Viz.

1. Sampson Lane 12. Joseph Terrell
2. James Tait 13. Tho[s] Mayfield
3. Reuben Shotwell 14. Richard Gray
4. Boley Conner 15. Joseph Chandler
5. Sterling Chandler 16. Benj[a] Cleveland
6. Joseph Reed 17. Deveroux Jarrett
7. John E. Carson 18. Joseph Walter
8. Anthony Story 19. Edm[d] King, J[r]
9. Foweler F. Adrine 20. Elias Burges
10. W[m] Pool 21. James Mitchell
11. W[m] Thomas 22. Henry Smith
23. Asa Allen
24. W[m] Hackett

October Term 1816

Pettit Jury N[o] 1

1. Reuben Baxter 7. Benjamin Wofford
2. Samuel Burton 8. Nathan Pitchford
3. William Tucker 9. James Reed
4. Thomas Davis 10. Charles Cawthon

5. Lembord King   11. Wm Lowrey
6. Saml Dailey   12. Wm Westbrook

George Haynie   }
    vs   } Case
Jeremiah Milner }

Jury N° 1

We find for the plaintiff two Hundred & fourteen Dollars, with interest & Costs.

                                            Charles Cawthon, Foreman

Ex^ors of Wm Hooper, D^d }
William Hooper   }
    vs   } Case
Rigdon Brown   }

Jury N° 1

We, the Jury, find for the plaintiff the Sum of One hundred and thirty five dollars, with Interest & Cost of Suit.

                                            Charles Cawthon, Forman

The State }
    vs   } Ind^t murder
William A. Blackburn }

True Bill.   Sampson Lane, foreman

October Term 1816

John E. Carson, in right of }
his wife and as agent for }
Nancy Hunter, Caviators }
    vs   } Caveat
Nancy [smudge] et alia }
[smudge] Ex^{ors} of } Richd Wood,
D^r }

appeal Dismissed.

Robert Barnhill }
    vs   } Trespass
Isham Medcock }

Jury N° 1

We, the Jury, find for the defendant, with Cost of Suit.

                                 Charles Cawthon, forman

The State   }   vs
} Ind^t Petit Larceny Wm H. Jordan
}

True Bill.   Sampson Lane, forman

The Court then adjourned untill to morrow morning Eight O'Clock.

Test. Maxfield H. Payne, Clk

Ex^d Young Gresham

October Term 1816

The Court met according to adjournment on tuesday 15th October 1816. Present, His Honor Judge Gresham.

John Johnston & wife }
    vs   } Trespass
James McDonald   }

We, the Jury, find for the defendant, with Cost of Suit.

                                    Charles Cawthon, Fm

John Johnston & wife }
    vs   } Trespass
James McDonald   }

We, the Jury, find for the defendant, with Cost of Suit.

                                    Charles Cawthon, foreman

Pettit Jury Nº 2
    1. Greenberry Sewell   7. John Carrell
    2. M̶[smudge] B̶o̶x̶ Elias Jordan   8. Wyly Hogwood
    3. George King   9. Charles Baker
    4. Wm Eddins   10. George Gober
    5. Frederick Holley   11. James Haley
    6. Peter Cockerban   12. Calob Garrisson

October Term 1816

Henry Mann   }   vs
} Trespass
Michal Redwine & }
Nelson Osburn   }

Dismissed.

The State   }   vs
} Indt murder
Elizabeth Lowry }

True Bill.   Sampson Lane, foreman

John Doe, ex Dem   }

John Mays } vs } Ejectment
Richard Roe &   }
Abisha Camp & }
Jesse Putman,

Tenants in possession }

appeal by Consent.

The State   }   vs
} Petit Larceny Wm Adams
}

No Bill.   Sampson Lane, foreman

Peter Grovor }
    vs   } Trespass
Dennis Phillips }

We, the Jury, find for the plaintiff fifty Dollars Damages & Cost of Suit.

                              Charles Cawthon, foreman

October Term 1816

The Court then adjourned untill to morrow morning Eight O'Clock.

Test. Maxfield H. Payne, Clk

Ex^d Young Gresham

The Court met according to adjournment Wednesday the 16th October 1816. Present, his Honor Judge Gresham.

Wm Crenshaw }
    vs   } Attachment Franklin Superior Court
Adam Cloud & } October Term 1816
John W. Cloud }

On motion of Counsel for the plaintiff, Stating that the Original attachment in the above Case, together with the negro levied on by the Same, was placed in the hands of the Sheriff of this County at the last Term of this Court & that he has failed to return the Same into this Court, to which the Same was made Returnable. It is therefore ordered, that the Sheriff Shew Cause to morrow morning at 9 O'Clock, or as Soon thereafter as Counsel

}

October Term 1816

can be heard, why he does not return Said attachment into Court, with his actings thereon.

Benjamin Dorsey }
    vs   } Debt
John P. Carnes }

I confess Judgment in favour of the plaintiff in this Case for the Sum of two hundred & forty dollars & fifty Cents, with interest and Cost of Suit.

                                Green W. Smith, Deft's attorney

The State } vs } Ind^t murder
Wm A. Blackburn }

Jury Sworn

1. Frederick Holley	7. Elias Jordan
2. Samuel Burton	8. Calob Garrisson
3. George King	9. David Mitchell
4. Wm Eddins	10. John Chalmers
5. Wm Lowry	11. Zachariah Chandler
6. John Halcomb	12. John Clark

This Case not got through with; it is Suspended untill to morrow.

October Term 1816

The Court then adjourned untill to morrow Eight O'Clock.

Test. Maxfield H. Payne, Clk

Ex^d Young Gresham

The Court met on Thursday According to adjournment, the 17th October 1816. Present, his Honor Judge Gresham.

The State }
    vs   } Ind^t murder
Wm A. Blackburn } Jury Sworn as yesterday

We, the Jury, find the Prisoner Guilty of the Charge alledged against him.

                                  Caleb Garrison, Forman

The Court then adjourned untill to morrow morning Eight O'Clock.

Test. Maxfield H. Payne, Clk

Ex^d Young Gresham

The Court met according to adjournment On Friday the 18th October 1816. Present, his Honor Judge Gresham.

Franklin Superior Court Oct. Term 1816

On motion of James Smith, attorney for William Wood, Stating that he has filed in the Clerk's office of this Court a Copy of a note Given by Thomas Harrington to Tryon Patterson and from him indorsed to William Wood, and evidence that the Original is lost. It is thereupon Ordered, that Said Copy be established in lieu of the Original upon this rule being published six month in a public Gazette in this State, if no person Should Shew Cause to the Contrary to this Court within Space of time.

The State } vs
} Ind^t murder
Wm A. Blackburn } Sentence

You, William A. Blackburn, are to be taken from this Bar to the Common Joal of this County, where you are to remain in Safe & Close Confinement untill friday the fifteen day of November the present year, & between the hours of ten O'Clock in the forenoon & three O'Clock in the afternoon of that day, you are to be

---

October Term 1816

Taken from thence by the proper Officer to a Gallows to be erected within the Vicinity of Carnesville, when & where you are by the like Officer to be hund by the neck untill you are dead, & may the God of Heaven have mercy On your Soul.

The State } vs
} Ind^t murder
Elizabeth Lowry } Jury Sworn

    1. William Burt   7. John Holcom
    2. George Carrell   8. Thomas Nunn
    3. William Martin   9. Reuben Baxter
    4. Zachariah White   10. Lemberd King
    5. William Baker   11. George King
    6. Thomas White   12. William Eddins

We, the Jury, do find the prisoner not Guilty.

                          Wm Martin, foreman

October Term 1816

The State } vs
} Ind^t Assault
James Ramsey }

True Bill.   Sampson Lane, forman

The State }
   vs   } Ind^t Assault
John Trigg }

True Bill.   Sampson Lane, foreman

The State   }
   vs   } Ind^t Assault
James Ramsey }

True Bill.   Sampson Lane, forman

The Grand Jury, in Common with their fellow Citizens, deeply lament the depravity and moral Corruption, which buts two, plainly appears to exist in our County at the present time and which has required the attention of the Court A considerable part of the present Term and we fondly hope that the Honorable Court will never experience So painful a duty in this County as has been required of him during the present Term. having no presentments to make, the Grand Jury beg leave to express their approbation of the assiduous discharge of his

---

October Term 1816

official duties by Judge Gresham & to tender him their thanks.
         S^{pn} Lane, foreman

Edm^d King, J^r	Wm Poole
Asa Allen	Wm Thomas
Thomas Mayfield	Joseph Chandler
John E. Carson	Benjamin Cleveland
James Tate	Deveraux Jarrett
Reuben Shotwell	Jo^s Walters
Boley Conner	Elias Burges
Starling Chandler	Ja^s Mitchell
Joseph Reed	Henry Smith
Anthoney Story	Wm Hackett

Georgia   }   The State }
Franklin County }   vs   } Ind^t murder
                          Eliz Lowry } Verdict not Guilty

This day Came in open Court John Lowry, the Husband of the prisoner, who being Duly Sworn, deposeth and Saith that he is unable to pay the Cost of the prosecution in the above Case, or any part thereof, and that he has not money, property,

---

or effects Sufficient to the discharge thereof, and that he has not disposed or Conveyed away the Same for the purpose of avoiding the payment of the Said Costs and Charges.

Sworn to & Subscribed in   }
Open Court 18th Oct 1816 }   John Lowry Test.   Maxfield H.
Payne, Clk }

The prisoner is Ordered to be discharged.

The Court then adjourned until to morrow Eight O'Clock.

Maxfield H. Payne, Clk

Ex^d Young Gresham

The Court met according to adjournment on Saturday the 19th October 1816. Present his Honor Judge Gresham.

___

Grand Jurors Drawn for April term 1817.

1. Benj^a Cleveland	19. Freeman Hardy
2. Royal Bryan	20. John McIntire
3. Wm Cawthon	21. Thos Anderson
4. Thos D. Jordan	22. Neely Dobson
5. Thos Payne A.	23. Richard Hooper
6. Reuben Payne	24. [smudge] Carrell
7. George Stovall, Esqr	25. Edmund Henly
8. Darby Henly, Esqr	26. James H. Little
9. John Mays	27. Seth Strange
10. Thos Lenoir	28. Joseph Chandler, B. C.
11. Moses Liddle	29. Caleb Griffith
12. Wm Ash, J^r	30. John Duncan
13. Robt Barnwell	31. Wyat Cleveland
14. John Hooper	32. Saml Payne
15. Timothy Terrell	33. Robert Hackett
16. Wm Ward	34. Richard Hutcherson
17. John Bush	35. Saml Headen
18. Hugh B. Greenwood	36. Robet Bevins

___

Pettit Jurors Drawn for April Term 1817

1. John Sewell	25. Sanford Gorham
2. Ric^d Ford	26. Lewis Moulder
3. Wm Barnhill	27. Jno Brown, S^n
4. Willis Seales	28. Jo^s Dickerson
5. Baker Ayers	29. Ja^s Smith
6. John Pearce	30. Jno Temples
7. Kinneth Finley	31. Jo^s Nickson

8. Alx. F. Ash
9. John Rucker, Jn^r
10. Richd Davison
11. Hez Smith
12. Ge° Taylor
13. Thos Hill
14. Jesse Brawner
15. Ge° Williamson
16. Jo^s McGrady
17. Larkin Holt
18. Thos Harbor
19. Henry Avery
20. [smudge] Baker
21. Thos Garrison
22. John Williams
23. David Crider
24. Starling Strang
32. John Nickson
33. Jesse B. Hansford
34. Jn° Wright
35. Tyre Swit
36. David Miller
37. Robt R. Cox
38. Jn° Barton
39. David Morgan
40. Edm^d Lovin
41. John Post
42. Henry Boroughs
43. Joel Hunt
44. Jo^s Whitehead
45. Jacob Pricket
46. Enock Andrews
47. Ja^s Armstrong
48. Clevery Philips

The State } Franklin Superior Court October Term 1816
vs } Indictment Petit Larceny Wm H. Jordan }

plea of Guilty Sentence

You, Wm H. Jordan, are to be taken immediately from this Bar to the whiping post erected in the Village of Carnesville & there by the proper Officer you are to receive on your bare back with a whip or Cowskin ten lashes & be thence discharged on payment of Cost.

Wm Crenshaw }
    vs } Atta Franklin Sup^r Curt Oct. Term 1816
Adam Cloud & }
John W. Cloud }

On motion of Counsel for plaintiff, Stating that the original attachment in the above Case has been lost or mislaid by the Sheriff of this County so that the same Can not be docketed at this term, to which it was returnable. It is therefore ordered, that the Defendants, or their Attorney, shew cause on the first day of the next term, or as soon thereafter as Counsel cane be heard, why the Case should not be docketed

---

& a sworn Copy established in lieu of the lost original Attachment.

I have rec^d notice of the above.   S. Upson

John Ivy } vs } Case

William Page } Jury

Sworn.

    1. Reuben Baxter   7. Caleb Garrison
    2. Samuel Burton   8. Nathan Pitchford
    3. Charles Baker   9. James Reed
    4. Thomas W. Davis   10. Charles Cawthon
    5. Lambard King   11. William Lowry
    6. Samuel Daily   12. Wm Westbrooks

We, the jury, find for the Plaintiff one hundred Dollars, with interest & Costs.

                      Charles Cawthon, foreman

Murray & Bryce }
    vs   } Case
Dudley Jones }

I Confess Judgment to the Plaintiffs for the Sum of Two Hundred thirty three dollars & twenty five Cents, with interest at seven per Cent on the Same up to the date the defendant ~~the defendant~~ shews he applied to McKinne in Augusta, agent of the plaintiffs, say April eighteen hundred & eleven, to pay the money, subject to the Opinion of the Court, as to the interest on the above Sum from the date of the said application to McKinne to the present date. In the argument of which point, the Counsel are to rely upon the general principle as to liability for interest at all. Plaintiffs are not to avail themselves of the above argument to pay interest up to April eighteen hundred & eleven in the argument.

                      Thomas W. Cobb, Atto for Deft

John Ivy, assignee }
    vs   } Case
Francis Williams }

Jury N° 1

We find for the plaintiff seventy five dollars, with Interest & Cost.

                      Charles Cawthon, forman

John Martin }
    vs   } Case
John Tate   }

Jury N° 1

We, the Jury, find for the plaintiff two hundred dollars, with Cost of Suit.

                      Charles Cawthon, forman

Henry Avery, assignee } of
Boley Conner, adm^r } of Eli
Bryan, Dec^d } vs   }
Case &C
William Studly &   }
James Blair   }

And now at this term comes the Defendant, James Blair, by his attorney, & do Confess Judgment to the plaintiff for the Sum of Fifty five dollars, with interest and Cost of Suit. Oct. Term 19th Octr 1816.

          Polydore Naylor,
          Atto for James Blair

John Doe, ex dem   }
Richard Roe   }   vs
} Ejectment
Salley Thrasher &   }
Benj^a Thrasher, } tenants
in possession }

Nonsuit.

The State } Franklin Superior Court vs }
October Term 1816
John English } Indictment for petit Larceny

Sentence

You, John English, are immediately to be taken from the bar by the proper Officer to the whipping post erected in the Village of Carnesville, & there by the like officer, with a whip or Cowskin, you are to receive on your bare back ten lashed & be discharged on payment of Cost.

The Court then adjourned untill Court in Course.

Maxfield H. Payne, Clk

Ex^d Young Gresham

George Haynie   }
  vs   } Case
Jeremiah Milner } & Verdict for plaintiff

And now Comes the Defendant, Jeremiah Milner in this Case, into Office, who being dissatisfied with the verdict in the above Case, has paid up the Cost an prayed an appeal, and at the Same time James Hooper, Jᵣ came with him and, as Security, Jointly and Severally acknowledged himself bound unto the plaintiff, George Haynie, for the final Condemnation money and Costs, as witness our hands & Seals This 23ʳᵈ October 1816.

Acknowledged before }
me & appeal Granted }
Maxfield H. Payne   }

Jeremiah Milner
James Hooper

April Term 1817

The Superior Court of Franklin County met according to adjournment, it being the Second Monday in April 1817 and also the 14ᵗʰ day of Said Month. Present His Honor Judge Dooly.

According to the Exigence of a writ of Venire to him directed, the high Sheriff of Said County returned said writ into Court, with the following persons Summoned and Sworn as Grand Jurors.

1. James H. Little
2. Royal Bryan
3. Wᵐ Cawthon
4. Thoˢ D. Jordan
5. Reuben Payne
6. Thoˢ Lenoir
7. Moses Liddle
8. Wᵐ Ash, Seʳ
9. Robert Barnhill
10. John Hooper
11. Timothy Terrell
12. Wᵐ Ward
13. John McIntire
14. Neely Dobson
15. Edmund Henley
16. Joseph Chandler
17. Seth Strange
18. Samˡ Payne
19. Robert Hackett
20. Samˡ Headen
21. George Stovall
22. Hugh B. Greenwood
23. John Mayes

April Term 1817

John Ivy   }
vs   } fi fa
William Page }

John Ivy, assignee }
   vs   } fi fa
Francis Williams }

On motion of Consel, it is ordered, that the Sheriff Shew Cause to morrow morning Eight O'Clock, or So Soon there after as Counsel can be heard, why he does not pay over the money on the above fi fas.

Pettit Jury Nº 1

1. Baker Ayers
7. Lewis Molder

2. John Pearson
3. Hezekiah Smith
4. Jesse Brawner
5. Thomas Hill
6. Sandford Gorham

8. John Temples
9. John Nixon
10. Joseph Nixon
11. Alex^r F. Ash
12. John Wright

William Tucker }
    vs   } assault & Battery
Robert Skelton & } & false imprisonment
John Sammond   }

Jury N° 1

We find for the Defendant, with Cost of Suit.

                                Sandford Gorham, fr^m

April Term 1817

Absalom Camron }
vs } False Imprisonment Joseph Barr }

Dismissed.

Barna, McKinne & Co }
vs   }
J. & Thos Hollingsworth }

Jury N° 1

We find for the plaintiffs one hundred and Sixty five dollars & thirty Six Cents, with interest & Cost.

                                Sandford Gorham, forman

Isaac Strickland }
    vs   } Debt
John D. Terrell & } John
Neal   }

Jury N° 1

We, the Jury, find for the Plff five hundred and fifty dollars & fifty Cents, with Interest & Cost of Suit.

                                Sandford Gorham, form^n

The Trustees of the }
University   }

vs } Debt
William Black }
Jury N° 1

We find for the plaintiffs Thirteen dollars thirty four Cents, with Cost.

         Sandford Gorham, for^m

Doctor Edward D. Smith }
 vs } Case &C
John T. Ralston }

Jury N° 1

We, the Jury, find for the plff thirty dollars, with interest & Cost of Suit.

         Sandford Gorham, forman

———

April Term 1817

Inferior Court }
 vs } Debt &C
Joseph Jones & }
Martin Jones }

Settled at Defendants' Cost.

Thomas Harbor, Henry Avery, Thomas Garrison, John Williams, John Brown, Junr, Joseph Dickerson, Tyre Swife, David Morgan find five dollars each.

Henry Brewer }
 vs } Trespass &C
William Hearndon }

Jury N° 1, with the exception of Alex^r F. Ash, Richard Chandler in his place.

We, the Jury, find for the plaintiff the sum of Three Dollars, with Cost of Suit.

         Sandford Gorham, forman

Richard Chandler }
 vs } Trespass &C
Joseph Chandler }

Jury N° 1

We, the Jury, find for the plaintiff twenty five dollars, with Cost of Suit.

         Sandford Gorham, forman

April Term 1816

Pettit Jury N° 2

1. Starling Strange
2. Henry Burroughs
3. Joel Hunt
4. James Armstrong
5. Cleverly Phillips
6. Richard Chandler
7. Wm Chandler
8. Joseph Reed
9. Benjn Tucker
10. John Barton
11. John Chandler
12. Peter C. Ballenger

The State } vs
} Ind^t Assault
David Connally & }
Elijah Christian }

True Bill.

Ja^s H. Little, forman

The State } vs } Ind^t Larceny
Benjamin Cooper & }
Hardiman Bennett }

True Bill.   Ja^s H. Little, forman

James Ramsey }
    vs   } Assault
John Trigg   }

Jury N° 2

We, the Jurors, find for the plaintiff five dollars, with Cost of Suit.

Jo^s Reed, foreman

April Term 1817

Jeremiah Sparks }
    vs   } Ca Sa
Abner Langford } Habeas Corpus

The Sheriff, having returned on this Writ that he has the body of the defendant in Open Court, with the cause of his detention, to wit, a Capias ad Satisfaciandon from under the hand and Seal of Wm Hackett, Esquire, for the Sum of forty five dollars & ninety three Cents with Costs, which is a greater Sum than the Justice of the peace has Jurisdiction of by the Constitution and Laws of the State, and it not appearing that the Said Ca Sa has been executed by any Offier whatever. It is ordered, that the Said Abner Lankford be discharged from his confined on both the Grounds above Stated, at the plaintiff's Cost.

The Court then adjourned untill to morrow morning Eight O'Clock.
Test. Maxfield H. Payne, Clk

Ex^d Jno M. Dooly

April Term 1817

The Court met according to adjournment 15th April 1817 at Eight O'Clock. present his Honor Judge Dooly.

Dudley Jones   }
    vs   } Debt
Absalom Cleveland }

Jury N° 1

We, the Jury, find for the plff the Sum of Seventy one dollars thirty Seven and a half Cents, with interest & Cost of Suit.

                            Sandford Gorham, forman

Inferior Court   }
    vs   } Debt
Thomas Morgan   }
Samuel Morgan &   }
Zebulon Garrison }

Jury N° 1

We, the Jury, find for the plaintiff the Sum of Six hundred and forty two Dollars and eighty five and three fourth Cents, with Cost of Suit.

                            Sandford Gorham, forman

Beach & Thomas   }
    vs   } Case &C
Wm A. Blackburn }

Settled at plffs Cost.

Benjn Dorsey   }
    vs   } Ca Sa
John P. Carnes   }

On motion of Consel for plaintiff, it is ordered that the Sheriff return the above casa into Court with his actings and doings thereon, or Shew Cause to the Contrary, this evening at 3 O'Clock.

April Term 1817

John Ivy } vs } fi
fa Wm Page }

John Ivy, assignee }
    vs   } fi fa
Francis Williams }

The Sheriff, being called upon this morning to Shew cause by Eight O'Clock why the money has not been Collected in the above Cases and paid to the plffs atto, Shews for cause that the Said executions has never been placed in his hands and they were not issued in time to be Served as he Knew of.

                                    Wm Beall, Shff

Sampson Lane }
    vs   } Case &C
James Glascock }
& Leroy Glascock }

Jury N° 1

We, the Jury, find for the plaintiff Sixty three dollars & Seventy two & ¾ cents, with Cost of Suit.

                                      Sandford Gorham, forman

John Doe, ex dem }
Heirs of Jesse Horn }
    vs   } Ejectment
Richard Roe & }
Thomas Nunn & }
Edward Ryly, tenants } in
possession }

Jury N° 1

We find for the plaintiffs the premises in dispute, with Costs of Suit.

                                      Sandford Gorham, form

April Term 1817

Inferior Court }
    vs   } Debt and
Thomas Morgan } Verdict for plaintiff
Samuel Morgan & }
Zebulon Garrison }

And now Comes the defendants in this Case, Thomas Morgan, Samuel Morgan, & Zebulon Garrison, Came into Court, who being dissatisfied with the Verdict in the above Case, has paid up the Cost and payed an appeal, and at the Same time Fleming F. Adrine came with them and, as Security, Jointly & Severally acknowledged himself bound unto plaintiff, the Inferior Court, for the eventual Condemnation money & Cost, as Witness our hands & Seals this 15th day of April 1817.

acknowledged before }   Thos Morgan me and appeal   }
Fleming F. Adrine Granted   }

Maxfield H. Payne, Clk

April Term 1817

Dox ex dem }
Frederick Bealls }
   vs   } Ejectment
Roe, Casual Ejector }
Robert Ramsey, } in
possession   }

Nonsuit.

John Trigg }
   vs   } Trespass
James Ramsey }

Dismissed.

The State   }
vs   } Ind^t Aslt
Greenbery Baker, }
otherwise Call^d } Green
Baker   }

True Bill.   Ja^s H. Little, Forman

The State   }
   vs   } Aslt
Green Chandler }

No Bill.   Ja^s H. Little, Forman

Dudley Jones, appett }
   vs   } Case
Benjamin Dorsey, Respt }

Jury Sworn.
     1. Royal Bryan   7. Edmund Henley

2. Thomas Lenoir	8. Samuel Payne
3. Moses Liddle	9. George Stovall
4. John Hooper	10. John Mayes
5. Wm Word	11. Caleb Griffith
6. Neely Dobson	12. Robert Hackett

We, the Jury, find for the plaintiff one hundred and twenty five dollars, with Cost of Suit.

Robert Hackett, foreman

April Term 1817

William Armstrong, Claimant }
vs }
The adm^{rs} of W^m McCracken, Dec^d }

Jury N° 1, with the alterration of John Barton in the place of Thomas Hill.

We, the Jury, find for the Claimant, William Armstrong, the mare Claimed, with Cost of Suit.

Sandford Gorham, forman

Farley Thompson, appett }
    vs } Trespass vi et armis
Isaac J. Barrett, Respt } Special
Jury Sworn.

1. Royal Bryan	7. Neely Dobson
2. Thos D. Jordan	8. Edmund Henley
3. Moses Liddle	9. Seth Strange
4. John Hooper	10. Saml Payne
5. William Ward	11. Hugh B. Greenwood
6. John McIntire	12. Caleb Griffith

We, the Jury, find for the original Plaintiff One hundred & Eighty dollars, with Cost of Suit.

N. Dobson, foreman

April Term 1817

Barna, McKinne & C° }
    vs } Debt &C
J. & Thomas Hollingsworth } Verdict for plaintiffs

And now comes the defendants, Thomas Hollingsworth, in this Case into Court, who being dissatisfied with the Verdict in the above Case, has paid up the Cost and prayed an appeal, and at the same time James Blair came with him and, as Security, Jointly &

Severally acknowledged himself bound unto the plaintiffs, Barna, McKinne, & C°, for the eventual Condemnation money & Cost, as Witness our hands & Seals this 15th April 1817.

acknowledged before }
me and appeal }
Granted }
Maxfield H. Payne, Clk

Thos Hollingsworth
James Blair

Joseph Dickerson, one of the Pettit Jury was find five dollars yesterday, is excused by filing an affidavit.

The Court then adjourned untill to morrow morning Eight O'Clock.

Test. Maxfield H. Payne, Clk

Ex^d Jn° M. Dooly

April Term 1817

The Court met according to adjournment Wednesday the 16th April 1817, present his Honor Judge Dooly.

The State }
     vs } recognizance for Perjury & passing los[smudge]
Jn° Bridges }

On motion of Counsel for John Bridges, stating that at the last Term notice was given to the So^l Genl that, unless the said Bridges should be prosecuted at this Term, they would move for his discharge, & the So^l Genl not now being able to prosecute.

Ordered, that the said John Bridges be discharged from his Recognizance.

Alexander Neal }
     vs } Certiorari James
Brown }

Sustained & a new trial ordered below.

William Hightower }
     vs } Debt
John Barton }

We find for the plaintiff twenty dollars, with interest & Costs.

                                       Sandford Gorham, forman

April Term 1817

Christopher Baker }
    vs   } Debt
Boley Conner   }

Dismissed.

The State   }
    vs   } Aslt
Peter Watters }

                          James H. Little, forman

True Bill.

The State } vs } Larceny
Stephen Brumley }

True Bill.   Ja^s H. Little, forman

The State } vs } Forgery
Andrew Collins }

No Bill.   Ja^s H. Little, forman

The State   }
    vs   } Aslt
John Chandler }

No Bill.   Ja^s H. Little, forman

The State   }
vs } Ind^t Petitit Larceny Joshua Hooper }

Jury N° 1

We, the Jury, find the prisoner at the bar guilty.

                          Sandford Gorham, foreman

——

April Term 1817

~~Grand Jurors Drawn for October 1817~~

Boley Conner, appett }
    vs   } Case &C
John R. Brown, Respt } Special
Jury Sworn.
       1. James H. Little   7. Timothy Terrell
       2. Wm Cawthon   8. Wm Ward

3. Thos D. Jordan	9. John McIntire
4. Thos Lenoir	10. Neely Dobson
5. Moses Liddle	11. Edmund Henley
6. John Hooper	12. Seth Strange

We, the Jury, find for the Plaintiff Seventy two dollars Six & ¼ Cents, with Cost of Suit, Provided property Belonging to the Estate of Eli Bryan, deceased, to that amount is or may hereafter come into the Possession of the defendant.

                                              James H. Little, foreman

Jeptha Yarbrough   }
Plaintiff in Execution }
      vs   }
Margaret Turk &   }
Wm Turk, Claimant }

Jury Sworn

1. James H. Little	7. Wm Ward
2. Royal Bryan	8. Neely Dobson
3. Wm Cawthon	9. Samuel Payne
4. Thos D. Jordan	10. Robert Hackett
5. John Hooper	11. George Stovall
6. Timothy Terrell	12. Richard Hutcherson

We, the Jury, find the property Subject to the Execution, during the Natural life of Margarett Turk, the defendant.

                                                James H. Little, foreman

---

~~April Term 1817~~

Joseph Ratchford, applt   }
     vs   } Bill in Equity
Larkin Cleveland, Ex respt }

In this case, the parties in Interest having come to a friendly adjustment of the matters in Controversy. On their Joint motion, the Case is entered Settled at the Costs of the defendant, who is the executors of Larkin Cleveland, decd, & named in the writs of Scire facias, & the ~~Executors~~ Execution for Costs to be Staid untill the next Term.
The Court then adjourned untill to morrow morning ~~Eight~~ Seven O'Clock.

Test. Maxfield H. Payne, Clk

Exd   Jno M. Dooly

[next two pages blank]

April Term 1817

The Court met according to adjournment 17th April 1817, present his Honor Judge Dooly.

Grand Jurors Drawn for October 1817.

1. Edm^d King, J^r
2. Charles Sisson
3. Thos Hollingsworth
4. Nathl Wofford
5. Lowry Gillaspie
6. Joseph Payne
7. Dudley Jones
8. Joshua Hudson
9. John Warmack
10. Joseph Reed, Esqr
11. Richd Allen
12. James Tait
13. Hugh Davidson
14. Saml Shannan
15. Samson Lane
16. Elias Burgess
17. Asa Allen
18. Redfern Weems
19. Abner Dunnagin
20. Anthony Story
21. Chris Baker
22. John Riley
23. Reuben Shotwell
24. Joseph Morris
25. John Mayfield, J^r
26. Robert Neale
27. Moses Gest, Esqr
28. Richd Say
29. Robt Bruce
30. Thos Mayfield
31. Gab^l Martin
32. Ja^s Martin, Esqr
33. Garrett L. Sandwick
34. Isaac J. Barrett
35. Saml H. Everett
36. James Allen, Esqr
37. David Payne
38. Ben Cleveland
39. Wm Hulsey
40. Jno Mullin

April Term 1817

Pettit Jurors Drawn for October 1817

1. Wm Smith, B. L.
2. Price Reissun
3. Thos Davis, J^r
4. Eli Shankley
5. Thos Savage
6. Ja^s Dawdy
7. John Holbrook
8. Elisha Lowry
9. Ben Prewit
10. John Townsend
11. Thos Mays
12. Ja^s Sewel
13. Thos Smith
14. John Mercer
26. Chris Denman
27. Robert Skelton
28. Ed Edwards
29. Charles Ishaw
30. James Lendsey
31. Saml Morgan
32. Stephen Chatham
33. Enock Brady
34. Thos Gober
35. Pat Mabrey
36. Wm Leath
37. John McDow
38. Chas Toney
39. Wm Reich

15. Henry Davis
16. Wm Flannagin
17. Thos Askew
18. Jer^h Sparks
19. Thos Story
20. Spencer Harrison
21. Woodson Roberts
22. Wm Chatham
23. Robert McFarlin
24. Atkins Tabor
25. Job Brooks

40. Benjⁿ Highfield
41. James Reed, S^r
42. John Crump
43. Wm Gest
44. Levi T. Taylor
45. Jesse Putman
46. Jno Denman
47. David Anthony
48. Adam Andrews
49. Ja^s Lowry, J^r
50. Jno Barber

Venire facias issued & delivered to the high Sheriff 19th April 1817.

April Term 1817

John Mays }
    vs   } Case
James Johnston }

Settled at Plff's Cost.

Dudley Jones }
    vs   } Case
Eli Tollison   } Bail

Settled.

Washington Allen }
    vs   } Special Case Warren
Stow   }

Nonsuit.

William Crenshaw }
    vs   } attachment
John W. Cloud & }
Adam Cloud   }

Exceptions being taken to this attachment & Sustained by the Court, it is order that the Same be dismissed.

The State   }
    vs   } Ind^t Pettit Larceny
James McIntire }

Jury N° 1

We, the Jury, find the prisoner at the bar not guilty.

        Sandford Gorham, forman

April Term 1817

The Grand Jury feel a pride in announcing to their fellow Citizens that a Very Small portion of their time have been Necessarily implode in Passing on Bills of Indictment during the present Term.

We also feel Equally gratified in not having any presentments to make on the Irregularities of our fellow Citizens.

Lastly, we, as the Grand Inquest for the County of Franklin, feel it a duty incumbent on us to Request his honor the Judge to except the highest assurance of our unfeigned thanks and Gratification in his faithful and unremitted attention to the discharge of his duty during the present Term.

James H. Little, Foreman	N. Dobson
Royal Bryan	Edmund Henley
William Cawthon	Seth Strange
T. D. Jordan	Joseph Chandler
T. Lenoir	Saml Payne
Moses Little	Robert Hackett
John Hoop	Saml Headen
Timothy Terrell	George Stovall
Wm Ward	H. B. Greenwood
Jno McIntire	Jno Mays
	Richard Hutcherson

April Term 1817

Isaac Strickland }
  vs   } Judgment
John D. Terrell & } John
Neal }

One of the Defendant, to wit, John Neal, comes into Court, payes up the Cost, & prays a Stay of Execution Sixty day, also comes Thomas Cox & Thomas Wilkins [smudge] acknowledges themselves equally bound unto the plaintiff, with the Defendant John Neal, on the Stay as above Stated. In witness whereof, we have Set our hands and Seals this 17th of April 1817.

Maxfield H. Payne, Clk

John Neal
Tho⁵ X Cox, his mark
Tho⁵ X Wilkins, his mark

The State } vs } Ind^t Petit Larceny
Joshua Hooper } Verdict Guilty

Sentence of the Court

That you, Joshua Hooper, be taken from this bar forthwith to the public whipping post in the Village of Carnesville and there receive on your barr back with a Switch or Cowskin by the proper officer three Lashes and to be thence dischargedon the payment of the Costs of this prosecution.

Thos Gorham }
     vs   } Certiorari
Wm Smith }

Dismissed and proceeding below Confirmed.

April Term 1817

The Adm^{rs} of }
Amos Bratcher, dec^d }
    vs   } Trover
John Westbrook }

A Rule Nisi having been obtained heretofore against the plaintiffs to Shew cause why a new trial Should not be Granted and no Sufficient cause now being Shewn.

It is ordered, that Said Rule be and the Same is now made absolute, on the ground that the Release Signed by One of the plaintiffs and tendered in evidence on the trail was improperly [blank]

The Adm^{rs} of }
Amos Bratcher, appts }
    vs   } Trover
Stephen Westbrooks, Respts }
Verdict for Respt at Oct. Term 1814. Rule Nisi for a new Trial Granted.

A Rule Nisi having been Granted, on a hearing, it is ordered, that the Said Rule Nisi be [smudge] now made absolute on the Second & fourth Grounds contained in the Said Rule Nisi and a New Trial be had in the Said Cause, according to the provisions of the Act in Such Case made & the Practice of Courts.

April Term 1817

Benjamin Dorsey }

vs } Case for Nuisance & verdict
Dudley Jones } for plff

On motion of Counsel for the Defendant, Ordered that the Plaintiff do Shew Cause, on the first day of the next Term, or so soon thereafter as Counsel can be heard, why a new trial Should not be Granted in the above Case on the following Grounds.

1st That the Verdict is Contrary to Law.

2nd That the Verdict is Contrary to evidence.

3rd That the Verdict is Contrary to the principles of Justice & Equity.

Thos W. Cobb & Walton Harris
attys for Deft

Murray & Bryce } Confession and question reserved as to
vs } liability of Deft to pay interest upon
Dudley Jones } a Bill of Goods furnished in New York at 6 months

This question having been argued, It is ordered, that the plaintiff have leave to Calculate interest on Said demand at the rate of 7 pr ct up to this time, and to sign Judgment according.

April Term 1817

James Hanna } vs
} Certiorari
Clemond Quillian, Esqr }
& Wm Elliott }

Sustained and new Trial ordered.

James Brown }
    vs } Certiorari April Term 1817
Isaac Brown }

On motion of Counsel for James Brown, it is ordered, that Caleb Griffith do make out a return to the above Case on or by the first day of next Term, or Shew Cause why an attachment Shall not issue against him for his neglect and that this rule be Served on the Said Caleb Griffith at least 20 days before the next Court.

Green W. Smith

The Court then adjourned untill Court in Course.

Exd   Jno M. Dooly

Maxfield H. Payne, Clk

April Term 1817

Richard Chandler }
    vs   } Trespass &C
Joseph Chandler } Verdict for plff

And now comes the Defendant, Joseph Chandler, into office, who being dissatisfied with the Verdict in the above Case, has paid up the Cost and prayed an appeal, and at the Same time Edmund Henley Came with him and, as Security, acknowledged himself Jointly and Severally bound unto the plaintiff, Richard Chandler, for the eventual Condemnation money & Costs, as Witness our hands & Seals this 18th day of April 1817.

acknowledged before me }   Joseph Chandler and appeal Granted
}   Edmund Henley
Maxfield H. Payne, Clk }

October Term 1817

The Superior Court of Franklin County met according to adjournment, it being the Second monday in October 1817 and also the 13th day of Said month. Present, His Honor Judge Dooly.

according to the Exigence of a writ of Venire to him directed, the high Sheriff of Said County Returned Said writ into Court with the following persons Summoned & Sworn as Grand Jurors.

1. James Allan   12. ~~Anthoney Story~~ James Tate
2. Thos Hollingsworth   13. Joseph Morris
3. Charles Sisson   14. John Mayfield, J^r
4. Joseph Payne   15. Moses Guest
5. Joshua Hudson   16. Richard Say
6. Hugh Davidson   17. Robert Bruce
7. Sampson Lane   18. Thomas Mayfield
8. Elias Burges   19. Gabriel Martin
9. Asa Allen   20. Garrett L. Sandrige
10. Redfearn Weems   21. Saml H. Everett
11. Abner Dunagan   22. David Payne
                            23. Reuben Shotwell

October Term 1817

Pettit Jury N° 1

1. Wm Smith   7. Thos Gober
2. John Holbrook   8. Wm Scott
3. Thos Smith   9. John McDow
4. Wm Chatham   10. Charles Toney
5. Robert McFarlin   11. Wm Rich
6. Christopher Denman   12. David Anthoney

John Miller, who was bail for Benjamin Cooper, at this term having delivered Said Cooper into Court & thereon was discharged.

James Whordlow }
& wife   }
    vs   } Trespass vi et armis
Benjamin Vines }

Dismissed.

Richard Smith, ex dem } of
Newell Walton   }
    vs   } Ejectment
William Stiles   }
Asa Langston, tenant }
in possession   }

Jury N° 1

We, the Jury, find for the plaintiff the premises in dispute, with Cost.

William Chatham, forman

October Term 1817

Pettit Jury N° 1

1. Wm Smith   7. Thos Gober
2. John Holbrook   8. Wm Scott
3. Thos Smith   9. John McDow
    4. Wm Chatham   10. Charles Toney
    5. Robert McFarlin   11. Jesse Thomas
    6. Christopher Denman   12. David Anthoney

Rachel White }
vs } Trespass vi et armis Miles Smith }

Jury as above in this Case.

We, the Jury, find for the plaintiff twenty dollars, with Cost of Suit.

John McDow, forman

John Rucker }
    vs   } Case
John Sutton }

Jury N° 1

We, the Jury, find for the plaintiff the Sum of fifty dollars, with interest and Cost of Suit.

John McDow, foreman

Moses Shannon }
    vs   } Slander
James Starrett }

Dismissed.

Robert H. Watkins }
    vs   } Debt
Presley Christian }

Jury N° 1

We, the Jury, find for the plaintiff the Sum of One hundred & Sixty nine dollars & fifty One Cents, with interest & Cost of Suit.

John McDow, forman

October Term 1817

Hugh Crawford }
    vs   } Debt
Ephraim B. Osbarn }

Jury N° 1
We, the Jury, find for the plaintiff the Sum of Sixty dollars, with Interest and Cost of Suit.

John McDow, forman

Pettit Jury N° 2

    1. John Denman   7. Benjamin Plaster
    2. Enoch Brady   8. Joseph Lewellen
    3. Henry Davis   9. Jesse Holbrook
    4. Adkins Tabor   10. John Bryan

    5. Elijah Sparks   11. William Clark
    6. Calbert Guest   12. George Longmire

State   }
   vs   } Sci fa vs^s the Bail
George Turman }
Edmund Henley }
Joseph Chandler }
& Boley Conner }

On motion of Counsel for Edmund Henley, Joseph Chandler, & Boley Conner, Stating that they were Bail for the Said George Turman, & that they now have their principal in Court, & wishes to Surrender him in discharge of their Recognizance. It is ordered, that the Said George Turman be taken into Custody by the Sheriff, & that the Said Edmund Henley, Joseph Chandler, & Boley Conner be & they are hereby exonerated from their liability in this Case.

October Term 1817

Darby Henley }
vs } Debt

Wm Turk }

Jury N° 2

We, the Jury, find for the plaintiff the Sum of Seventy dollars twelve & half cents, with Interest & Cost of Suit.

                                                         John Bryan, F. M.

Henley & Bush & C° }
vs } Debt Wm Turk   }

We, the Jury, find for the plaintiff Eighty dollars, with Interest & Cost of Suit.

                                                         John Bryan, F. M.

Beach & Thomas   }
   vs   } Debt
Wm A. Blackbourn }

Jury N° 2

We, the Jury, find for the plaintiff the Sum of fifteen hundred & twenty one dollars & Eighty Seven Cents, With Interest & Cost of Suit.

                                                         John Bryan, F. M.

John Doe, Ex dem } Nathan
Smith   }

vs } Eject
Richd Smith & }
Simon Terrell }

Jury N° 1

We find for the defendant the premises in dispute, with Cost of Suit.

John McDow, foreman

Jabez Jones, adm^r
} of Joshua Yowell
}
   vs } Debt
Beverley Greenwood }

Jury N° 1

We, the Jury, find for the plaintiff the Sum of Six hundred & Seventy Six dollars, With Interest & Cost of Suit.

John McDow, foreman

October Term 1817

John E. Carson }
   vs } Debt
John Trigg }

Jury N° 2

We, the Jury find for the plaintiff forty dollars, With Interest & Cost of Suit.

John Bryan, F. M.

Hanslu Payne }
   vs } Case
Richard Dabbs }

Jury N° 2

We, the Jury, find for the plaintiff Seventy dollars, with Interest & Cost of Suit.

John Bryan, F. M.

Joseph Taylor }
   vs } Debt
John Knox, J^r }

Jury Nº 1

We, the Jury, find for the plaintiff the Sum of forty dollars and twelve and a half Cents, with interest and Cost of Suit.

         John McDow, foreman

William Clark }
 vs   } Case
John Trigg }

Jury Nº 1

We, the Jury, find for the plaintiff the Sum of forty One dollars, with interest & Cost of Suit.

         John McDow, foreman

David Barnett }
 vs   } Debt
John Gilley }

Jury Nº 2

We, the Jury, find for the plaintiff thirty dollars & thirteen Cents, with interest & Cost of Suit.

         John Bryan, F. M.

Wiley Dyer   }
 vs   } Debt
Jeremiah Milner & }
Thoˢ P. Buroughs }

Settled.

October Term 1817

The State }
vs } Assault
Henry Davis }

True Bill.   James Allan, Forman

The State } vs } Assault
Parnal Tindal }
Sally Tindal   }
Robert Alexander }
Mathew Alexander }

True Bill.   James Allan, Forman

The State   }
    vs   } Aslt
Elijah Fleming }

No Bill.   James Allan, forman

John Doe, ex dem   }
Holloway & Wells Carnes } by
their next friend }
Richd Carnes   }   vs   }
Ejectment
Richard Roe &   }
Sally Thrasher & }
Benedict Thrasher,   }
tenant in possession   }

Dismissed.

Dudley Jones }
 vs } Debt Wm Page }

Settled.

Dudley Jones,   } assignee of W^m
B. Bryan }
    vs   } Case
William Studley &   }
James B. Cain   }

Settled.

October Term 1817

Exd   Jn° M. Dooly

The Court then adjourned untill to morrow morning nine O'Clock.

Maxfield H. Payne, Clk

The Court met according to adjournment 14th October 1817. Present, his honor Judge Dooly.

Georgia, Franklin County Superior Court

October Term 1817

Patience Tolbert } by her
next friend } &
Father William Aaron }
    vs } Libel for a divorce
Washington Tolbert }

The Sheriff having Returned that the Defendant is not to be found in this County. It is therefore, on motion of Benjamin Wilson, Attorney for the plaintiff, ordered that Service be perfected by publishing this order Once a month for three months in the Georgia Journal.

The Heirs of Edward Palmer }
vs } Ejectment Joel Yowel }

Jury N° 1

We, the Jury, find for the Defendant, with Cost of Suit.

                                      John McDow, foreman

October Term 1817

N° 1

1. Wm Smith   7. Thos Gober
2. John Holbrook   8. Enoch Brady
3. Thos Smith   9. John McDow
4. Wm Chatham   10. Charles Toney
5. Henry Davis   11. Wm Rich
6. Christopher Denman   12. David Anthoney

The Inferior Court of Franklin County, that is to say, Asa Allen, Edmund Henley, James Hooper, Joseph Chandler, & John E. Carson.
Franklin Sup^r Court Debt appeal we, the aforementioned members of the Said Court, do hereby agree that the above Case may be dismissed at the defendant's Cost, given under our hands Seals, this 13th day of October 1817.

                                      Asa Allen, J. I. C.
                Edmund Henley, J. I. C.   James Hooper, J. I. C.

John Mays }
    vs } Ejectment & appeal by consent
Abisha Camp & }
Jesse Putman }

On motion of counsel for plaintiff, it is ordered, that the Sheriff Shew cause to morrow morning at nine O'Clock, or so soon thereafter as counsel can be heard, why the Costs which have been collected in this case Should not be refunded.

October Term 1817

Green Chandler }
  vs   } Trespass vi et armis
Greenberry Baker }

Jury Nº 1

We, the Jury, find for the plaintiff twenty five dollars, with Cost of Suit.

            John McDow, foreman

Nancy Reynolds &   } Nimrod Leathers, in
} right of his wife,   } appellants   }
vs   } Trover & Conversion
George Turman, Respondant } Jury Sworn.

  1. James Allan   7. Robert Bruice
  2. Asa Allan   8. Thos Mayfield
  3. Abner Dunagan   9. Gabriel Martin
  4. Joseph Morris   10. Saml H. Everett
  5. John Mayfield   11. David Payne
  67. Richard Say   12. Reuben Shotwell

We, the Jury, find for the plaintiff Four thousand dollars, with Costs of Suit, which may be discharged by delivering the Negroes, together with Such other of the property mentioned in the decleration as is now in existence to the Plaintiff, or his Attorney, within thirty days.

            James Allan, Foreman

The State } vs } Perjury
Jonathan Box }

True Bill.   James Allan, foreman

October Term 1817

Benjamin Plaster }
  vs   } Debt
John Trigg   } Bail

The Defendant, John Trigg, being Surrender in Court by his Bail, Brings Stephen Dixon, who acknowledges him Selve bound [blot] for the Defendant, John Trigg, ~~for the eventual condemnation money & Cost~~ as Special Bail in Said Case.

In witness whereof, we have hereunto set our hands & Seals this 14th October 1817.

Maxfield H. Payne, Clk   John Trigg, Stephen Dickson

Joseph Taylor }
    vs   } Debt & Verdict
John Knox, J^r }

The Defendant, John Knox, J^r, comes into Court & prays a Stay of Sixty days, also comes Christopher Denman and acknowledges him Self bound unto the plaintiff with the defendant, John Knox, J^r, on the Stay as above Stated, which Stay was Granted on payment of Cost.

Maxfield H. Payne, Clk   Jo^h W. Knox, Ju^n

                                                Christopher Denman

Inferior Court   }
    vs   } Debt
Thomas Morgan   }
Samuel Morgan &   }
Zebulon Garrison   }

Dismissed at Appelt's' Cost.

October Term 1817

Jonathan Baugh is fined twenty five dollars & is confined till paid.

Philip Fagan is fined twenty five dollars to be confined till paid.
Ex^d Jno M. Dooly

The Court then adjourned untill to morrow morning nine O'Clock.

Maxfield H. Payne, Clk

The Court met according to adjournment 15th October 1817.

Maxfield H. Payne, Clk. Present, his Honor Judge Dooly

Joseph Ratchford   }
    vs   } Equity
The Executors of   }
Jesse Walton, Dec^d }

On motion of Counsel. It is ordered, that the Clerk Shew cause instanter why he Does not issue an Execution for the Cost in the above Case under the Settlement.

October Term 1817

Richard Smith, ex dem } of
Newell Walton }
    vs } Ejectment & Verdict for Plaintiff
William Stiles }
Asa Langston, tenant }
in possession }

And now comes the Defendant into Court, who being dissatisfied with the Verdict in the above Case, has paid up the Cost & prayed and appeal, and at the Same time comes John Bush with him and acknowledged him Self Jointly and Severally bound unto the Plaintiff, Newell Walton, for the eventual condemnation money & Cost.

In Witness whereof, we have hereunto Set our hands & Seals this 15th day of October 1817.

Maxfield H. Payne, Clk   Asa Langston, John Bush

The Heirs of Edward Palmer }
    vs } Ejectment Joel Yowell }

Jury N° 1

We, the Jury, find for the Defendants, with Cost of Suit.

                                       John McDow, foreman

The fines of Jonathan Baugh & Philip Fagan are remitted.

October Term 1817

John E. Carson }
    vs } Debt
John Trigg }

William Clark }
    vs } Case
John Trigg }

The Defendant, John Trigg, comes into Court, pays up the Cost in both the above Stated Cases, and prays a Stay of Execution Sixty days, also comes Elias Jordan & Larkin

Perdu with him and acknowledges them Selves Jointly & Severally bound to the plaintiffs for the Judgment.

In testimony whereof, we have Set our hands & Seals this 15th October 1817.

Maxfield H. Payne, Clk   John Trigg
                                Elias Jordan

                                Larkin X Perdu, his mark

James R. Haley }
      vs   } Certiorari
John Beasley }

Verdict below Set aside & new trial ordered.

The State   }
    vs   } Ind^t Ast
John Cleveland }
True Bill.   James Allen, foreman

The State   }
    vs   } Ast
Robert Hackett }

True Bill.   James Allen, foreman

October Term 1817

The State   }   vs
} Ind^t Larceny
Stephen Brumley }

Jury Sworn.
    1. Wm Smith   7. Thos Gober
    2. John Holbrook   8. Wm Scott
    3. Thos Smith   9. John McDow
    4. Wm Chatham   10. Charles Toney
    5. Robert McFarlin   11. Wm Rich
    6. Christopher Denman 12. David Anthoney

We, the Jury, find the prisoner at the Bar not Guilty, but A malicious prosecution and the prosecutor to pay the Cost.

                                John McDow, forman

William Irby } vs } Trespass vi et armis
Jonathan Baugh &   }
Mary Baugh, wife } of the
Said Jonathan }

Settled at mutual Cost.

Ex^d   Jn° M. Dooly

The Court then adjourned until to morrow nine O'Clock.

Maxfield H. Payne, Clk

October Term 1817

The Court met according to adjournment 16th October 1817. Present, his Honor Judge Dooly.

Pettit Jury N° 1 as to day

1. Wm Smith   7. Enoch Brady
2. John Holbrook   8. Thos Gober
3. Thos Smith   9. John McDow
4. Wm Chatham   10. Charles Toney
5. Robert McFarlin   11. Henry Davis
6. Christopher Baker   12. David Anthoney

The State }
   vs   } Ind^t Misdemeaner
Edy Holbrook }

True Bill.   James Allan, forman

John Doe, ex dem }
John Mays   }   vs
} Ejectment Abisha Camp &
}
Jesse Putnam   }

Jury Sworn.
1. James Allan   7. Sampson Lane
2. Thos Hollingsworth   8. Elias Barges
3. Charles Sisson   9. Joseph Morris
4. Joseph Payne   10. Redfearn Wims
5. Joshua Hudson   11. Abner Dunagan
6. Hugh Davidson   12. James Tait

We, the Jury, find for the Plaintiff the premises in dispute, with Costs of Suit.

                                  James Allan, forma

October Term 1817

James C. Watson, et al }

vs } Equity
Isaac J. Barrett }
Bill for discovery & }
Ni ex eat }

Dismissed.

The State }
    vs } Indictment for Petit Larceny
Stephen Brumley }

On motion of Mr Cook, Attorney for the defendant, it is ordered, that the Clerk deliver to the defendant, or his attorney, a Copy of the bill of indictment & acquittal in the above Stated Case, to enable him to commence his action against the prosecutor for a malicious prosecution.

Hudson Moss, appl
} vs }
William B. Wofford, } Respondant
}

Jury Sworn.

    1. Joshua Hudson   7. John Mayfield
    2. Sampson Lane   8. Moses Guest
    3. Redfearn Weems   9. Robert Bruce
    4. Abner Dunnagan   10. Thos Mayfield
    5. James Tate   11. Gabriel Martin
    6. Joseph Morris   12. David Payne

We, the Jury, find for the Plaintiff One hundred Dollars, with Interest and Cost of Suit.

We further find the Sum of Ten pr Cent on the amount of the principal for delay.

                                    Jo Morris, foreman

October Term 1817

Grand Jurors drawn for April Term 1818.

    1. Thompson Moore   21. Joseph Chandler, B. C.
    2. Fred^k Beall   22. Joseph Reed, Esqr
    3. James Hooper, Esqr 23. John Duncan, Senr
    4. Simon Terrell   24. Wyatt Cleveland
    5. Wm Thomas   25. Caleb Griffith
    6. James Blair   26. Dudley Jones
    7. John Neal   27. John Mays
    8. Wm Pool   28. John E. Carson
    9. Wm Bush   29. Wm Hackett

10. Robert Barns
11. George Stovall, Esqr
12. Wm Cawthon
13. Robert Barnwell
14. Wm Hulsey
15. Edmund King, J^r
16. Samuel Headen
17. Darby Henley, Esqr
18. Anthoney Story
19. John Riley
20. Christopher Baker

30. Saml Payne
31. Nathl Wofford
32. Lowry Gillaspie
33. Thos Anderson
34. Deveroux Jarrett
35.
36.
37.
38.
39.
40.

October Term 1817

Pettit Jurors drawn for April Term 1818.

1. Jesse Smith
2. Nathan Bond
3. Livsey Anderson
4. Wm Holbrook
5. John Gasaway
6. John Beasley
7. Elijah Thornton
8. Reuben Thornton
9. Thos Conn
10. Absalom Tranham
11. Thos Towsen
12. Ben^j Plaster
13. Zebulon Garrison
14. Richard Brown
15. John Ivy
16. Abisha Camp
17. James Henderson
18. Wm Baker, J^r
19. Green Sewell, J^r
20. Elijah Sparks
21. Thos Farmer
22. James Mercer
23. Peter Jones
24. Ben^j Lowry
25. John Echols

26. David Mitchell
27. John Adrian
28. James Jackson
29. John Ayers
30. Wm Brown
31. John Brown
32. Chesley Cawthon
33. Jeptha White
34. Joshua Ward
35. David Lowry
36. H[smudge] Collier, J^r
37. Jacob White, J^r
38. Wm Blair
39. Allen Chandler
40. Wm Mitchell
41. Jack Gober
42. Arthur Taylor
43. John Bryan, J^r
44. Richard Molder
45. Benjamin Ashworth
46. James McCarter
47. Patrick Scott
48. John Downs
49. Wm Redwine
50. John Payne, J^r

Venire facias issued & delivered to the high Sheriff 20th October 1817.

October Term 1817

Polley Hamilton }
    vs   } Divorce
Joseph Hamilton } Jury
Sworn.

    1. James Allan   7. Moses Guest
    2. Charles Sessons   8. Richd Say
    3. Joshua Hudson   9. Robert Bruce
    4. Hugh Davidson   10. Gabriel Martin
    5. Asa Allen   11. Garrett L. Sandrige
    6. Joseph Morris   12. Reuben Shotwell

We, the Jury, find that Sufficient proof has not been refered to our consideration to authorize a divorce between the parties.

                              James Allan, Forman

John R. Brown   }
Plaintiff in execution }
    vs   } Claim
Boley Conner, admrs } of
Eli Bryan, dec^d }
Claiment   }

Dismissed.

James Brown }
    vs   } Certiorari
Isaac Brown }

Dismissed & proceeding Below Confirmed.

Elijah Sparks }
    vs   } Illegality
Charles Ward }

Sustained.

Reuben Higgin }
    vs   }   Illegality
Thomas Cox   }

Sustained.

October Term 1817

Jabez Jones, adm^{rs} of } Joshua
Yowell, dec^d }

   vs } Debt & Verdict for Plaintiff Beverly
Greenwood }

And now Comes the Defendant, Beverly Greenwood, into Court, who being dissatisfied with the Verdict in the above Case, [aid up the Cost & prayed an appeal, and at the Same time Comes Presley Christian with him and acknowledges himself Jointly and Severely Bound unto the Plaintiff for the eventual Condemnation money & Cost.

              [signature spaces blank]

Ex^d Jn° M. Dooly

The Court then adjourned untill to morrow morning ~~nine~~ Eight O'Clock.

Maxfield H. Payne, Clk

The Court met according to adjournment 17th October 1817. Present his honor Judge Dooly.

October Term 1817

William Cawthon }
  vs   } Certiorari
Jn° Allbritton }

On motion of Counsel for plaintiff, it is ordered, that the Justices Royal Bryan & George Stovall, Esqr make a further return to this Court at the next term, Stating particularly whether Isaac Allbritton only entered the appeal in his own name or as agent, and whether any & was the evidence on the part of John Allbritton on the trial of the Said appeal & whether any Offset was filed by him or evidence of payment or want of ~~payment~~ Consideration, and that this be Served twenty days before next term on the Said Justices.

Deloney Williams }
  vs   } Libel for Divorce Franklin Superior Court Nancy
Williams   } Oct. Term 1817

The Sheriff, having returned that the deft is not to be found in the county, on motion of counsel for the libelant, it is ordered that the deft do appear at the next term of this court & plead to the libel or the court will proceed as in cases of judgment by default & that this order be published in one of the public gazeets of this state three months previous to the next superior Court to be held in and for said county.

October Term 1817

Fountain Thurmond }
  vs   } In Equity
William B. Wofford }

On motion of Solicitor for Complainant. It is ordered, that the defendant doth plead, answer, or demur, not demurring alone, on or before the Second day of the next Term, or the Bill be taken pro confesso.

William Scott }
    vs   } In Equity
William Goodwin }

On motion of Counsel for Complainant. It is ordered, that the defts plead, answer, or demur, not demurring alone, on or before the first day of the next term, or the Bill be taken pro Confesso.

Wm Milweed wife }
    vs   } In Equity
The Exr^s of Alexander Williamson } Bill for Account & Legacy

On motion of Complainant's Solicitor, it is ordered, that the Defendant doth plead, answer, or demur, not demurring alone, on or before the Second day of next Term, or the bill be taken Pro confesso.

John   Simmons }
vs   }
Victor Smith   }

Settled at Defent's ~~plffs~~ Cost.

October Term 1817

Murray & Brice }
vs   }
Dudley Jones   }

On motion of Counse Stating to the Court, that in this case the confession of the party a judgment has been obtained & that the Same has not been Signed. It is ordered, that the plff's attorney have leave to Sign Judgment Nune Pro Tunk & issue execeution accordingly.

Franklin County }
October Term 1817 } The Grand Jury for the County aforesaid present as a grivance the evasion or violation of the law intended to prohibit the importation of Slaves into this State for Sale.

We present as a grievance the bad Situation in which the public roads Generally in this County are Kept. And trust that the officers whose duty it now is to Superintend them will attend more particularly to their duty.

We present the following persons for retailing Spiritous liquors without license from this County, viz, Harris Toney, James Fleming, Samuel H. Everett, John Simmons,

Michael Box, Junr, Simon Satter, James Gilbert, James Bagley, Samuel Haden, John Knox, James Morris, and Thomas W. Davis.

October Term 1817

We request his honor to appoint commissioners to examine into the State of the County funds and direct them to report thereon to the next Grand Jury and beg leave to recommend Sampson Lane, Joseph Morris, and James Allan for that purpose.

We return our thanks to his Honor Judge Dooly for the assiduity and attention paid by him to his official duties during the present term.

We request that the above be published in the Georgia Journal.

James Allan, Foreman	James Tait
Thomas Hollingsworth	Joseph Morris
Charles Sisson	John Mayfield, Junr
Joshua Hudson	Richard Say
Hugh Davidson	Robert Bruce
Sampson Lane	Thomas Mayfield
Elias Burgess	Gabriel Martin
Asa Allen	Garrett L. Sandige
Redfern Weems	Reuben Shotwell

The presentments of the Grand Jury being taken up. It is ordered, that Sampson Lane, Joseph Morris, & James Allan be and they are hereby appointed to examine

---

October Term 1817

into the State of the County funds and report to the next Grand Jury pursuant to the request in Said presentments Contained, also that the Clerk do transmit a Copy of Said presentments for publication.

The Heirs of Edward Palmer }
    vs   } Ejectment
Joel Yawel, Tenant in possession } Verdict for Deft

Duncan G. Campbell, the plffs attorney, being dissatisfied with the verdict in the above Case, Came forward and prayed an appeal to a Special Jury, which is Granted. And the Said D. G. Campbell and Elizabeth Palmer enter themselves Security for the eventual Condemnation money and all future Costs, the Costs due up to this time being first paid.

Maxfield H. Payne, Clk   Duncan G. Campbell
                                                                   E. Palmer
Ex^d Jno M. Dooly

The Court then adjourned untill Court in Course.

Maxfield H. Payne, Clk

Ex^d Jn° M. Dooly

October Term 1817

Green Chandler }
  vs   } Trespass & Verdict
Greenberry Baker }

The Defendant Comes into Office, pays up the Cost in the above Case, & prays a Stay of Execution Sixty days, and at the Same time Comes Christopher Baker, Junr and acknowledges himself bound for the principal & Interest on the Stay. In testimony whereof, I have Set my hand & Seal this 21st day of October 1817.

Maxfield H. Payne, Clk   Christopher Baker

Jabez Jones, adm^r } of
Joshua Yowell }
  vs   } Debt
Beverly Greenwood } Verdict for Plff

And now comes the Defendant, Beverly Greenwood, into office, who being dissatisfied with the Verdict in the above Case, has paid up the Cost & prayed an appeal, and at the Same time came Presley Christian with him and acknowledges him Self Jointly & Severally bound unto the plaintiff for the eventual condemnation money & Cost, in testimony whereof, I have hereunto my hand & Seal this 21st day of October 1817.
Maxfield H. Payne, Clk   Presley Christian, Beverly Greenwood

---

April Term 1818

The Superior Court of Franklin County met according to adjournmet on the Second monday in April, and also the 13th day of said month.

Present, His Honor Judge Dooly.

According to the exigence of a writ of Venire to him directed, the High Sheriff of said County returned said writ into Court with the following persons Summoned & Sworn as Grand Jurors.

  1. Frederick Beall   12. John Mays

  2. Thompson Moore   13. William Hackett

3. John Neal

4. George Stovall

5. William Cawthon

6. Robert Barnhill

7. Samuel Headen

8. Anthoney Story

9. Joseph Chandler

10. Joseph Reed

11. John Duncan

14. Lowry Gillaspie

15. Jesse Thomas

16. Robert Barns

17. Dudley Jones

18. Joseph Walters X

19. John E. Carson

20. Darby Henley

21.

22.

23.

Robert Smith, ex dem }
Robert Barns }   April Term 1818
    vs }   } Ejectment
John Doe }
Averet Shuffield, ten^t } in
possession }

Pettit Jury N° 1

    1. Nathan Bond
    2. Wm Holbrook
    3. John Beazley
    4. Elijah Thornton
    5. Reuben Thornton
    6. Thos Conn

    7. Absalam Trantham
    8. Benjn Plaster
    9. Green Sewell
    10. James Mercer
    11. Peter Jones
    12. Benjn Lowry

William Irby }
vs }
Jonathan Baugh }

Settled at Defendant's Cost.

William Hearndon }
 vs } Trespass Jacob Cox }

Settled at Defendant's Cost.

Willis, Banks, & C° }
    vs   } Debt
Adam Clement   } & Richard Harden } Jury N° 1 we, the Jury, find for the plaintiff Sixty Seven dollars, with interest & Cost.

                              Greenberry Sewell, foreman

April Term 1818

The State   }   vs
} Ind^t Hog Stealin
Benjn Tucker }
True Bill.   Fred^k Beall, Fm

The State   }
    vs   } Ind^t Assault
Robert Burton }

                              F. Beall, Forman
True Bill.

The State } vs } Ind^t Forgery
James W. Edward }

No Bill.   F. Beall, Forman

Washington Allen }
    vs   } Debt
Warren Stow   }

Jury N° 1 we find for the Defendant,

with Cost.

                              Greenberry Sewell, F. M.

Pettit Jury N° 1

       1. Nathan Bond   7. Absalom Trantham
       2. Wm Holbrook   8. David Mitchell
       3. John Beazley   9. Green Sewell
       4. Elijah Thornton   10. James Mercer
       5. Reuben Thornton   11. Peter Jones
       6. Elijah Spark   12. Benja^n Lowry

Stephen Russell }
    vs   } Debt
Saml Bright   }

Jury N° 1

We, the Jury, find for the plaintiff Eighty five dollars & twenty five Cents, with [blot]terest & Cost.

          Greenberry Sewell, Fm

April Term 1818

Benjamin Plaster }
  vs   } Debt
John Trigg   }

Jury N° 1

we, the Jury, find for the plaintiff One hundred & fifty Six dollars & Seventy Cents, with Interest & Cost.

          Greenberry Sewell, Fm

William Brown   }
  vs   } Debt
Nathaniel Wofford }

~~Jury N° 1~~

I Confess Judgment to the plaintiff for Sixty Six dollars & Sixty Six Cents, with Interest & Cost.

         Green W. Smith, Deft's Atty

Robert Taylor   }
  vs   } Case
Nancy Woods, Exor^x }
Samuel Shannon, Exo^r } James H. Little, Exo^r } of Richard Woods, Dec^d }

Jury N° 1 we, the Jury, find for the plaintiff Seven hundred and twenty five dollars, with Cost.

          Greenberry Sewell, Fm

Robert Burns   } agent
for John Cox }
  vs   } Attachment
Jonathan Box   }

April Term 1818

State }
   vs   } Recognizance for Keeping the peace. April Term 1818
Thomas Gilbert }
Lewis Moulder }

On motion of Counsel for defendants, Stating that the warrant on which the foregoing proceedings are founded is not directed to any lawful officer, or other person by name, to execute and return, and that there is no Oath or affidavit returned on which the warrant could be predicated, and the Solicitor General having acknowledged notice & not Gainsaying the Statement, and the Said George Aderhold not appearing to pray or Shew cause for continuance of the Recognizance. It is Ordered, that the Said Thomas Gilbert & Lewis Moulder be forthwith discharged on payment of Costs.

Ex^d Jn° M. Dooly

The Court then adjourned untill to morrow morning nine O'Clock.

Test. Maxfield H. Payne, Clk

The Court met accordind to adjournment 14th April 1818.

Maxfield H. Payne, Clk

April Term 1818

Pettit Jury N° 1

1. Nathan Bond	7. James Mercer
2. Wm Holbrook	8. Peter Jones
3. John Beazley	9. Benjn Lowry
4. Elijah Thornton	10. Thos Conn
5. Reuben Thornton	11. Greenberry Sewell
6. Absalom Trantham	12. Benjn Plaster

Robert Williamson }
   vs   } Case
Sampson Lane & } Matilda
Bagwell } admrs of
Winkfield } Bagwell, dec^d
}

Jury N° 1 we find for the plaintiff five hundred & fifty Dollars. With interest & Cost.

                               Greenberry Sewell, F. m.

Elijah Cherry }
    vs   } Trover & Conversion
Samuel Bright }

Jury N° 1

We find for the Defendant, with Cost of Suit.

                                  Greenberry Sewell, F. m.

April Term 1818

William Smith, et uxor }
vs } Bill for Discovery, relief, & Distribution John Neal & others }
adm^{rs} of Joseph Neal } Jury Sworn.

    1. Frederick Beall   7. Anthoney Story
    2. Thompson Moore   8. Joseph Chandler
    3. George Stovall   9. Joseph Reed
    4. Wm Cawthon   10. John Duncan
    5. Robert Barnhill   11. John Mays
    6. Samuel Hedden   12. Wm Hackett

We, the Jury, find for the Plaintiff the Sum of Six Hundred & Ninety nine Dollars & fifty five & three fourth Cents, with Cost of Suit.

April 14th 1818   F. Beall, F^m

James Smith, et uxor   }
    vs   } Bill for discovery, relief, & Distribution John
Nail & others   } adm^{rs} of Joseph Nail, dec^d }

Jury as above.

We, the Jury, find for the Complainents the Sum of ~~five~~ Six hundred & ninety nine dollars & fifty five & three fourth Cents, with Cost of Suit.

                                    F. Beall, Fm

John Epperson }
    vs   } Trespass vi et armis
Joseph Baker }
James Baker & }
Elias Baker   }

Jury N° 1

We find for the defendants, with Cost of Suit.

                                Greenberry Sewell, F. m.

April Term 1818

John R. Compty }
    vs   } Case for words John
Baugh }

Dismissed.

Wilson McKinney, assignee }
    vs   } Debt
William Legg }

Jury N° 1 we, the Jury, find for the plaintiff two hundred dollars, with interest & Cost.

                        Greenberry Sewell, F. m.

Terrell & Holley }
    vs   } Debt
William Wofford }

we, the Jury, find for the Plaintiffs the Sum of eighty dollars & seventy five Cents, with Interest & Cost.

                        Greenberry Sewell, Fm

Humphey Agee }
    vs   } Case
Ephraim B. Osborn }

I Confess Judgment to the plaintiff for fifty Six dollars four & three fourth Cents, with interest & Cost.

                        Green W. Smith, Deft's Atty

April Term 1818

The State } vs } Purjury
John Harmon }

No Bill.   F. Beall, Forman

Jesse Whipple }
    vs   } Case
Christopher Baker, Senr } Jury N° 1 we find

for the defendant, with Cost of Suit.

                        Greenberry Sewell, F. m.

John Brown }
    vs   } Trespass vi et armis
George Vaughan }

Jury N° 1

We, the Jury, find for the plaintiff two hundred and fifty dollars, with Cost of Suit.

                                Greenberry Sewell, F. m.

Ex^d Jn° M. Dooly

The Court then adjourned untill to morrow morning nine O'Clock.

Maxfield H. Payne, Clk

The Court met according to adjournment 15th April 1818.

Maxfield H. Payne, Clk

April Term 1818

Washington Allen }
    vs   } Deceit
Warran Stow   } Judgment for Defendant

The Plaintiff, being dissatisfied with the above Verdict, came into Court and prayed an appeal, and at the Same time comes Richard Allen with him and acknowledges him Self Jointly & Severally bound unto the defendant for the eventual Condemnation money & Cost.

Witness our hands & Seals this 15th day of April 1818.

Maxfield H. Payne   Washington Allen   Richard Allen

Daniel Beall &
Amos Bratcher, adm^{rs} }
of Amos Bratcher, Dec^d }
    vs   } Trover
John Westbrook   } Appeal & Originally Suit Dismissed

April Term 1818

Robert Williamson }
    vs   } Case and Verdict for plaintiff
Sampson Lane & } Matilda
Bagwell } adm^{rs} of W. F.
Bagwell }

now Comes Sampson Lane, One of the administrators in the above Case, for himself & Matilda Bagwell, who being dissatisfyed with the above ~~Judgment~~ Verdict, pays up the Cost & prays an appeal, which was Granted without Security, they being administrators.

                                          Sp^n Lane, adm^r

J. & Thomas Hollingsworth, Appellants }
            vs   }
Barna, McKinney, & C°, Respondents }

Jury Sworn.

    1. George Stovall   7. Lowry Gillespie
    2. Saml Headen   8. Jesse Thomas
    3. Anthoney Story   9. Robert Barns
    4. Joseph Reed   10. Dudley Jones
    5. John Duncan   11. John E. Carson
    6. Wm Hackett   12. Darby Henley

We, the Special Jury, find for the respondant One hundred & fifty two Dollars & twenty eight Cents, with Cost of Suit.

15th April 1815   Darby Henley, F. m.

The State   }
    vs   } Aslt
John Cleveland }

Jury N° 1

We find the Defendant Guilty of the assault only.

                                          Greenberry Sewell, F. m.

April Term 1818

The State   } vs }
Assault
Purnal Tindal   }
Sally Tindall   }
Mathew Alexander }

& Martha Alexander }

Purnal Tindal & Martha Alexander, two of the defends named in the above Bill, Came into Court with Mathew Alexander [blank], their Securities, and acknowledged themselves bound unto his Excellency Wm Rabun, governor for the time being, and his successors in office in the Sum of one thousand dollars, Conditioned to be void on Condition that the Said Purnal Tindal and Martha Alexander shall appear at the next term of this Court and shall not depart without leave thereof.

	Purnal Tindal
Octr 1818 Reconizance forfeited	Arthur Aldine
& Sci fa ordered	M. Alexander
D. G. Campbell, So^l Genl	Martha X Alexander, her mark

Richard Chandler }
    vs   } Case
Joseph Chandler }

Special Jury
    1. Fre^d Beall
    2. Thompson Moore
    3. John Neal
    4. George Stovall
    5. Wm Cawthon
    6. Robt Barnhill
    7. Saml Headen
    8. Anthony Story
    9. Joseph Reed
    10. John Denman
    11. John Mays
    12. Wm Hackett

We, the Jury, find for the respondent the Sum of Fifty five dollars, with Cost of Suit.

                                            Fred^k Beall, Forman

---

April Term 1818

The State }
    vs   } Aslt
Robt Burton }

Robert Burton and Alexander F. Ash and Eli Ramsey Came into Court and acknowledged themselves bound to his Excellency the gover for the time being in the Sum of One thousand dollars, for the payment of which they bind themselves, exr^s, adm^{rs}, &c.

Conditioned to be void if the Said Robert Burton shall make his personal appearance at the next term of this Court and shall not depart without leave of the Court & the order thereof, otherwise to be and remain in force & Virtue.

                                              Robert Burton

    Alex^r F. Ash   Ely Ramsey

The State } vs } Ind^t Hog Stealing

Benjamin Tucker }

Know all men by these presents that we, Benjamin Tucker, principal, and James Cary & William Smith, his Securities, are Jointly & Severally bound unto his Excellency William Rabun, Governor, & or his Successors in office, in the full & Just Sum of five hundred dollars, which payment will & truly to be made we bind ourselves, heirs, &C. The Condition of the above obligation is Such that, if the above bound Benjamin Tucker

———

does in his own proper person be & appear at the Superior Court now in cession, from day to day, untill from thence discharged by a due course of Law, then this obligation to be Void, Other wise to remain in full force & Virtue.

Given under our hands & Seals this 15th April 1818.

Maxfield H. Payne, Clk   Benjamin X Tucker, his mark
                                  James X Cary, his mark
                                  W^m Sm Smith

Ex^d Jno M. Dooly
The Court then adjourned untill tomorrow morning Eight O'Clock.

Maxfield H. Payne, Clk

The Court met according to adjournment 16th April 1818.

Maxfield H. Payne, Clk

The State } vs } Assault
Robert Hackett }

Robert Hackett find five dollars.

The above fine paid.

———

April Term 1818

Benjamin Dorsey }
    vs   } Verdict an Appeal for plff
Dudley Jones   } & motion for a new trial

At April Term 1818, Argument having been heard by the Court on both Sides upon the Grounds taken in the Rule Nisi for a new trial, & the Court being of Opinion that the verdict is contrary to evidence. It is ordered, that a New trial be Granted.

John R. Brown } plff in
Execution   }
    vs   } Illegality

Boley Conner, Claimant } dismissed &

the fi fa ordered to proceed.

The adm^{rs} of Thomas Grogg }
plff in Execution }   vs
}
Robert Brown, defent }
& John Brown, Claimt }

Jury Sworn.

1. Nathan Bond 7. James Denman
2. Wm Holbrook 8. Peter Jones
3. John Beazley 9. Benjamin Lowry
4. Elijah Thornton 10. Thos Conn
5. Reuben Thornton 11. Greenberry Sewell
6. Absalom Trantham 12. Benjamin Plaster

We, the Jury, find the land Subject, with ten per cent for delay.

Greenberry Sewell, fm

April Term 1818

The State }
    vs   } Assault upon a Slave
Thomas Mullins }
William Jackson }
Joseph Jackson }

True Bill vs Thomas Mullins & William Jackson. No Bill vs Joseph Jackson.

Fred^k Beall, forman

The State }
    vs   } Assault upon a Slave
Thomas Mullins }
& Wm Jackson }

Thomas Mullins, one of the defendants, and John Mullins, his Security, Came into Court and acknowledged themselves held and firmly bound to his excellency Wm Rabun, governor of this State for the time being, and his Successors in office, in the Sum of Five hundred Dollars.

Conditioned to be void if the above named Thomas Mullins shall appear at the next term of the Sup^r Court to be holden in this County to answer such things as shall be objected against on the part of said State for the above assault.

Test. Maxfield H. Payne, Clk   Thomas Mullin, Jno Mullin

April Term 1818

Georgia } Franklin County } To the Honorable the Judge of the Superior Court of Said County

The petition of John W. Hooper humbly Sheweth that your petitioner has for Some time been engaged in the Study of the law under the direction of Allen Lawhon, Esqr, your petitioner therefore prays that your Honor would Order that he may be examined and, if found qualified, that he may be admitted to the practice of the Law, and as in duty bound your petitioner will ever pray &C.

John W. Hooper

I Certify that Mr John W. Hooper has been engaged for Some time past in the Study of the law under my direction and that he is a Young Man of good Moral Character. I have every reason to believe that he is of the proper age for Admission.

Allen Lawhon, 13th April 1818

April Term 1818

Committee named So^l Genl Campbell, Mr Paine, Mr Gilmer, Mr Oliver.

The Committee have discharged their duty in the examination of the applicant and recommend his Admission.

D. G. Campbell, So^l Genl
Edward Paine
James Oliver
Ge^o R. Gilmer

I, John W. Hooper, do Solemnly Swear that I will well and truly demean myself as an Attorney, Solicitor, and Counsellor in the Several Courts of Law and equity in this State, that I will Support, maintain, and defend the Constitution of the ~~United~~ States of Georgia and the Constitution of the United States. So help me God.

Sworn to in Open Court }   John W. Hooper
This 16th April 1818   }
Maxfield H. Payne, Clk }

John W. Hooper, having petitioned the Court for examination as aforesaid and having passed an approved examination & this day also appeared in open Court and being publicly examined, which is Satisfactory to the Court, and having taken & Subscribed the foregoing Oath. It is ordered, that the said John W. Hooper be and he is hereby admitted to the practice of Law in the Several Courts of Law & Equity in this State.

April Term 1818

Deloney Williams }
    vs   } Libel for Divorce
Nancy Williams }   Jury
Sworn.

1. Frederick Beall	7. Samuel Headen
2. Thompson Moore	8. Anthoney Story
3. John Neal	9. Joseph Chandler
4. George Stovall	10. Joseph Reed
5. Wm Cawthon	11. John Duncan
6. Robert Barnhill	12. John Mayes

we find that Sufficient proofs have been referred to our Consideration to authorize a total divorce, that is to Say, a divorce a Vinculo matrimonii upon legal principles between the parties in this Case.

                                  F. Beall, Foreman

David Brogdon }
    vs   } Libel for Divorce
Sally Brogdon }

Jury as in the Case above.

We find that Sufficient proofs have been referred to our Consideration to authorize a total divorce, that is to Say, a divorce a vinculo matrimonii upon legal principles between the parties in this Case.

                                  F. Beall, Forman

Patience Tolbert, by   }
her next friend & Father }
Wm Aaron   }
    vs   } Libel for Divorce
Washington Tolbert   }

Jury as above.

We, the Jury, find Sufficient proofs have been referred to our consideration to authorize a total divorce, that is to Say, a vinculo matrimonii upon legal principles between the parties in this Case &C.

                                  Fred^k Beall, Forman

April Term 1818

The State } vs } Ind^t

Benjamin Tucker }

Jury Sworn.

1. Nathan Bond   7. James Denman
2. William Holbrook   8. Peter Jones
3. John Beazley   9. Benjamin Lowry
4. Elijah Thornton   10. Thos Conn
5. Reuben Thornton   11. Greenberry Sewell
6. James Mercer   12. Benjamin Plaster

We, the Jury, find the prisoner guilty.

          Greenberry Sewell, Fm

Georgia   }
Franklin County } We, the Grand Jury in & for the County aforesaid, Present His Honor Judge Dooly our Sincere thanks for his judicious attention during the present Term. And, at the Same time, feel gratified that we have no presentments to return.

April 16th 1818   Fred^k Beall, Fm

Halman Harbaun }
   Vs } Action ~~of Deceit~~ on the same ris Richard
White } nature of Deceit

Settled & costs paid.

Ralph Banks }
 vs } Case
Silas Crump }

Settled & cost paid.

~~Robert H. Watkins~~ } M.
T. Wilhite, adm^r }
 vs   } Case
~~Clyveland Lane~~ }
George Stovall }

Settled & cost paid.

Thomas Goolsby, for } the
use of James N. Brown }
 vs   } Case
William Goolsby, sur pro }
Nancy Glenn, Exr^x }
Simson Glenn & }

Wᵐ Goolsby, Exʳ }

Non Suit.

John Bryan } vs
} Attachment
Richard White } Dismissed.

Willis Newton }
    vs   } Trover
John Hooper }

For the purpose of making a Speedy & final, and of the above Case it is agreed that an appeal be now entered returnable to the next term & that the Case then, to wit, at the next Term, Stand for trial.

———

Jesse Whipple }
    vs   } Case Case
Christopher Baker, Cen }

In this case, Jesse Whipple, by John A. Heard, his attorney, came into court and paid all cost and prayed an appeal, an acknowledged himself, together with Willis Banks, his security, bound for all cost and damage Which may accrue in said case, on the final determination thereof. In testimony whereof, we have hereunto set our hands and seals this 16th day of April 1818.

Test. Maxfield H. Payne, Clk   John A. Heard, atty for Jesse Whipple
               Willis Banks

Exᵈ   Jnº M. Dooly

The Court then adjourned untill to morrow Eight O'Clock.

Maxfield H. Payne, Clk

———

William Smith, et uxor }
    vs   } Bill for Discovery &
John Neal & others   } & relief Distribution
admʳˢ of Joseph Neal } Verdict for plffs

James Smith, et uxor }
    vs   } Bill for Discovery &
John Neal & others   } relief & Distribution
admʳˢ of Joseph Neal } Verdict for plffs

John Neal, One of the Defendants in the above two Stated Case, being dissatisfied with the Verdict in each Case, Comes into office, pays up the Cost & prays an appeal, and at the Same time Comes Thomas Wilkins and acknowledged himself bound unto the plaintiffs for the eventual Condemnation money & Cost, in testimony whereof, we have hereunto Set our hands & Seals this 16th April 1818.

Maxfield H. Payne, Clk   John Neal   Thomas X
Wilkins, his mark

The Court met according to adjournment 17th April 1818.

Maxfield H. Payne, Clk

James Denman }
    vs   } Certiorari
John Bowman }

On motion of Counsel for plaintiff, it is ordered, that John Womack and Darius Echols, Esquires, Justices of the peace in the District of Capt Morris, do make a further & full return in the above Case having regard particularly to the matters Stated & complained of in the affidavit on which the Said Certiorari is founded & which is annexed to Said Writ, and that a copy of this be Served upon them thirty days before the Setting of next Court.

William Cawthon }
    vs   } Certiorari April Term 1818
John Allbritton }

Counsel having been heard in the Said Case, it is ordered and considered by the Court that the said Certiorari be Sustained, that the Justices of the Justices below be Confirmed, and that the appeal be dismissed on the ground that the said appeal was entered by Isaac Allbritton in his own name & not in the name of John Allbritton, the Defendant.

Benjamin Baker, for   } indorsey
of Saml Gloland }
    vs   } Debt
John Trigg   }

I confess Judgment to the plaintiff for Sixty Seven dollars & fifty Cents, with interest & Cost.

                                           John Trigg

April Term 1818

Grand Jurors Drawn for Octr term 1818

1. John McIntire
2. Thos Mayfield
3. H. B. Greenwood
4. Richard Hutcherson
5. Wm Ward
6. Neely Dobson
7. Hugh Davidson
8. Gabriel Martin
9. Robert Bruce
10. G. L. Sandigde
11. David Payne
12. James Martin, Esqr
13. Samul Shannon
14. Benjn Cleveland, S. C.
15. Wm Ash, Senr
16. Robert Neal
17. Benjn Cleveland
18. John Warmack
19. Joseph Payne
20. John Mayfield, J^r
21. Seth Strange
22. Edwd Carrell
23. Richd Allen
24. Henry Smith
25. Joshua Hudson
26. Richd Gray, Esqr
27. James Tate
28. Sampson Lane
29. Reuben Payne
30. Thos Hollingsworth
31. Timothy Terrell
32. Joseph Morris
33. Joseph Chandler, G. S.
34. Robert Hackett

Ann Ward &   }
John Ward   }
    vs   } Bill for discovery &C
Joseph Martin   }

Dismissed.

Petit Jurors Drawn for Oct Term 1818.

1. Ignatius Purcel
2. Moses Sewell
3. Larch Ganes
4. [blot] Williams
5. Robt Williams
6. Andrew Earwood
7. Ja^s Deff~~neur~~
8. Wm Wilkerson
9. Jo^s Dobins
10. Elisha Diar
11. Michael Box, J^r
12. Richd Shockley
13. Saml McKee
14. Richd Halcomb
15. Robt Walters, J^r
16. Ja^s Lowerey, J^r
26. Jesse Dabs
27. Jeremiah Taylor
28. Groves Yarbour
29. Burrell Whitehead
30. Aaron Sanders
31. Robt Crump
32. Jno Halcomb
33. David Thornton
34. Wm Tayler
35. Archabld Cockburn
36. Zach Mise
37. Jno P. Carnes
38. Robt Fleming
39. Drury Rose
40. Robt Chandler
41. Lenor Paxon

17. Jnº Vannum
18. Jaˢ Wilkenson
19. Geº Carrell
20. Wyatt Lankford
21. Wᵐ Fleming
22. Thoˢ Blair
23. Wᵐ Edwards
24. Thoˢ Cox
25. Henry Cannon

42. Jnº Sewell
43. Jaˢ Holingsworth
44. Benʲ Becham
45. Thoˢ Ivy
46. Josiah Sartin
47. Jaˢ Gober
48. Moses Trimble
50. Zach Chandler

venire issued & Given to the Sheriff.

April Term 1818

The State }
    vs   } Indᵗ Hogstealing
Benjamin Tucker } Verdict Guilty

You, Benjamin Tucker, are Sentenced to undergo an imprisonment in the Common Jail of the County of Franklin for the Space of two months, to Commence from this day. That you pay to the Clerk of this County for the use of Janus Nix the Sum of five dollars, being the Value of the property Stolen, and that you be thence discharged upon payment of the Costs of this prosecution.

Exᵈ   Jnº M. Dooly

The Court the adjourned Untill Court in Course.

Maxfield H. Payne, Clk

Richard Chandler }
    vs   } Trespass
Joseph Chandler }

The Defendant, Joseph Chandler, Came into Office, paid up the Cost, & prayed a Stay of Execution Sixty days, & at the Same time came Frederick Beall, his Security, & acknowledged himself Bound with the Defendant to the plaintiff for the amount of the Judgment & Interest. Given under our hands & Seals this 21ˢᵗ day of April 1818.

Maxfield H. Payne, Clk   Joseph Chandler, Fredᵏ Beall

Benjamin Plaster }
    vs   } Case
John Trigg   } & Verdict for plaintiff

The Defendant, John Trigg, came into Office and prayed a Stay of Execution Sixty days, & at the same time came Stephen Dixon, his Security, & acknowledged himself Bound to the plaintiff for the Judgment, interest, & Cost.

Given under our hands & Seals this 21st day of April 1818.

Maxfield H. Payne, Clk   John Trigg, Stephen Dickson

October Term 1818

The Superior Court of Franklin County met according to adjournment on the Second monday in October 1818, it being the 12th day of Said month. Present, His Honor Judge Dooly.

According to the exigence of a writ of Venire to him directed, the high Sheriff of Said County Returned Said Writ into Court, with the following persons Summoned as Grand Jurors.

Grand Jury

1. Sampson Lane, forman
2. John Mayfield
3. Edward Carrell
4. Thomas Mayfield
5. James Tate
6. Robert Hackett
7. Hugh B. Greenwood
8. Joshua Hudson
9. David Payne
10. John McIntire
11. Joseph Morris
12. Gabriel Martin
13. Richard Gray
14. Samuel Shannon
15. Benjamin Cleveland
16. Henry Smith
17. + Robert Bruice
18. Garrett L. Sandidge
19. James Martin
20. X William Ward
21. X Timothy Terrell
22. Richard Allen
23. John Warmack
24. Maj Benjamin Cleveland

October Term 1818

Petit Jury Nº 1

1. Nathl Williams
2. James Defurr
3. Wm H. Wilkinson
4. Joseph Dobbins
5. Saml McKee
6. Robert Walters
7. Groves Yarbrough
8. Burrell Whitehead
9. Aaron Sanders
10. Robert Crump
11. John Holcomb
12. Drury Rose

Thoˢ D. Jordan }
    vs   } Case
Jnᵒ D. Terrell & } G.
D. Paine   }

Jury Nº 1

We find for the plaintiff Eighteen Dollars thirty eight Cents, with interest & Costs.

                                    Samuel Mackee, Fm

William Foote }
    vs   } Debt
Stephen Kirk & }
David Mitchell }

Jury Nº 1

We, the Jury, find for the plaintiff one hundred and two dollars and thirty nine Cents, with interest and Cost of Suit.

                                      Samuel Mackie, Fm

Moses Haynes }
    vs   } Debt
Polydore Naylor }

Jury Nº 1

We find for the plaintiff forty One dollars & twenty three Cents, with interest & Cost.

                                      Samuel Mackie, fm

October Term 1818

Thomas Townsend }
    vs   } Debt
Charles Gilley & }
Darius Echols   }

Jury Nº 1

We, the Jury, find for the plaintiff the Sum of thirty five dollars, with interest and Cost of Suit.

                                      Samuel Mackie, foreman

John W. Freeman }

vs   } Case
Adam Clement & }
Richard Hardin }

Jury N° 1

We find for the plaintiff One hundred & twelve dollars and Seventy five Cents, with interest & Cost.

                                            Samuel Mackie, foreman

Wm Chambers }
   vs   } Debt
John Knox, J^r }

Jury N° 1

We find for the plaintiff fifty Dollars, with interest & Cost.

                                              Samuel Mackie, foreman

The State   }
vs   } Ind^t Burglary
Noah Smith }

True Bill.   Sampson Lane, Foreman

The State   }   vs
} Ind^t Assault
George W. O'Kelly }

True Bill.   Sampson Lane, Foreman

October Term 1818

Robert Bruce, Timothy Terrell, & Wm Ward Grand Jurors Sworn & excused.

The State } vs } Asl^t
Wm Sewel, Senr }

True Bill.   Sampson Lane, Fore^m

Absalom Harris }
      vs   } Case for word Allen
Smith   }

Nonsuit.

Robert Walters, J^r   }
   vs   } Trespass vi armis

Edward Swann, Senr }
Edward Swann, J^r }

Jury N° 1, Jeremiah Tayler in place of Robt Walters.

We, the Jurors, find for the plaintiff One hundred dollars, with Cost of Suit.

Saml Mackie, F. M.

Ex^d Jn° M. Dooly

The Court then adjourned untill to morrow morning nine O'Clock.

Maxfield H. Payne, Clk

October Term 1818

The Court met according to adjournment tuesday 13th October 1818. Present, his Honor Judge Dooly.

Maxfield H. Payne, Clk

Pettit Jury N° 1

1. Nathaniel Williams
2. James Defur
3. Wm H. Wilkinson Jeremiah Taylor
4. Joseph Dobbins
5. Samuel McKie
6. Burrell Whitehead
7. Aaron Sanders
8. Robert Crump
9. John Holcom
10. Thos Ivy
11. James Merrell
12. Drury Rose

The State }
vs } Larceny from the person John Reed }

True Bill.   Sampson Lane, forman

Pettit Jury N° 2

1. Robert Watters
2. Wm H. Wilkinson
3. Robert Chandler
4. John M. Smith
5. Wm Fleming
6. Moses Trimble
7. Zachariah Chandler
8. Groves Yarborough
9. Josiah Sartin
10. Ignatius Purcel
11. Hezekiah Smith
12. Wm Scott

October Term 1818

Robert Mitchel }
vs } Trespass vi et armis John Trigg }

Jury N° 1

We, the Jurors, find for the Plaintiff twenty Dollars, with Cost of Suit.

                                         Samuel Mackie, F. M.

Jeremiah Milner, app^t }
    vs   } Case
George Haynie, Resp^t }

Jury Sworn
    1. Edward Carrell   7. Gabriel Martin
    2. Thos Mayfield   8. Richard Gray
    3. Robert Hackett   9. Saml Shannon
    4. Hugh B. Greenwood   10. Benjn Cleveland
    5. John McIntire   11. Henry Smith
    6. Joseph Morris   12. Garrett L. Sandidge

We, the Jury, find for the Respondant the Sum of two hundred and thirty dollars, with interest and Cost, also the additional Sum of twelve and a half percent on the Principal Sum Due for delay.

                                         Joseph Morris, Foreman

The adm^{rs} of Amos Brather, applts }
vs   }
Stephen Westbrook, Resp^t }

October Term 1818

Robert Mitchell }
       vs   } Trespass John
Trigg   }

Jury N° 2

We, the Jury, find for the Plaintiff twenty five Dollars, with Cost of Suit. 13th October 1818

John M. Smith, Fm

Beverly Greenwood }
   vs }
Jabez Jones, adm^r of }
Joshua Yowel, Resp^t }

Jury Sworn.

  1. Sampson Laine   7. H. B. Greenwood
  2. John Mayfield   8. Joshua Hudson
  3. Edward Carrell   9. David Payne
  4. Thos Mayfield   10. John McIntire
  5. James Tate   11. Joseph Morris
  6. Robert Hackett   12. Gabriel Martin

We, the Jury, find for the Respondant the Sum of Six hundred and Seventy Six Dollars, with Interest at 7 per Cent, also the additional Sum of fifteen per Cent on the principal amount, with Cost of Suit.

            Sampson Lane, forman

October Term 1818

John Beck & Leroy Pope }
otherwise called   }
John Beck & Company }
  vs   } Case &C
Adkinson Tabor &   }
Acquillia Shockley,   }
adm^{rs} of Benjamin King, dec^d }

Settled at Defendants' Cost.

The State } vs } Larceny
Thomas W. Davis }
Wm H. Davis   }
Humphrey Agee }

No Bill. We, the Jury, believe this to be a malicious prosecution.

            Sampson Laine, Forman

The State }
 vs   } Affray
John Baird & }
John Bird }

True Bill.   Sampson Lane, Fm

James W. Edward }

vs } Assumpsit
Stephen Westbrook }

Dismissed.

James W. Edwards }
    vs } Assumpsit Drury
Rose }

Dismissed.

October Term 1818

William Stiles }
Asa Langston, }
Tenant in possession }
appellant } vs } Ejectment
Richard Smith, ex dem of }
Newell Walton, Respondant } Jury
Sworn.

    1. Sampson Laine   7. Hugh B. Greenwood
    2. John Mayfield   8. Joshua Hudson
    3. Edward Carrell   9. David Payne
    4. Thos Mayfield   10. John McIntire
    5. James Tate   11. Joseph Morris
    6. Robert Hackett   12. Gabriel Martin

We, the Jury, find for the plaintiff the premises in dispute, with Cost of Suit.

                                               Sampson Lane, foreman

Ex^d Jno M. Dooly

The Court then adjourned untill to morrow Nine O'Clock.

Maxfield H. Payne, Clk

October Term 1818

The Court met according to adjournment Wednesday 14th Octr 1818.

Maxfield H. Payne, Clk

Robert Walters }
    vs } Trespass &C
Edward Swann, Senr }

Edward Swann, J^r }

Edward Swan, Senr, One the Defendants in the above Case, being dissatisfied with the Verdict, came into Court, pays up the Cost, & prays an appeal, & at the Same time Came Peter Brown and acknowledged himself bound unto the plaintiff for the eventual Condemnation money and Cost. In witness whereof, we have hereunto Set our hands & Seals this 14th October 1818.

Maxfield H. Payne, Clk   Edwd Swann, Peter Brown

The Heirs of Edward Palmer, appl^t }
      vs   } Ejectment
Joel Yowel, Resp^t   }

Jury Sworn.
    1. Sampson Lane   7. Hugh B. Greenwood
    2. John Mayfield   8. Joshua Hudson
    3. Edward Carrell   9. David Payne
    4. Thos Mayfield   10. John McIntire
    5. James Tate   11. Joseph Morris   6. Robert Hackett
12. Gabriel Martin

we find for the defendant the premises in dispute, with Cost of Suit.

                                  Sp^n Lane, Foreman

October Term 1818

Pettit Jury N° 1, John Bowman in place Thos Ivy.

Pettit Jury N° 2, Thos Smith in place of Hezekiah Smith, Asa Ayers in place of Wm Scott.

The State }
vs } Ind^t Larceny from the person John Reed }

~~Jury Sworn.~~

John Reed arraigned & plead not guilty.

Jury Sworn.
    1. James Defur   7. Robert Walters
    2. Jeremiah Taylor   8. Robert Chandler
    3. Burrell Whitehead   9. John M. Smith
    4. Robert Crump   10. Thos Smith
    5. John Halcom   11. Joseph Yates

6. John Bowman   12. John Bellamy

We, the Jury, find the prisoner at the Bar guilty.

John M. Smith

Pettit Jury N° 1

1. Nathl Williams   7. Aaron Sanders
2. James Defur   8. Robert Crump
3. Jeremiah Taylor   9. John Holcom
4. Joseph Dobbins   10. John Bowman
5. Samuel Mackie   11. James Merrell
6. Burrell Whitehead   12. Drury Rose

October Term 1818

The State } vs } Assault
Purnal Tindal }

Jury N° 1

We, the Jury, find the defendant guilty of an assault.

Samuel Mackie, F. M.

The State } vs } Assault
Martha Allexander }

Jury N° 2

We, the Jury, find Martha Alexander guilty of the Charge Laid against her in this Bill of Indictment. October 14th 1818

John M. Smith, Fm

The State }
vs } Assault
Sally Tindall }

Know all men by these presents that we, Sally Tindall, principal, and Pernal Tindal & Mathew Alexander, her Securities, are Jointly and Severally bound unto his Excellency William Rabun, Governor, or his Successors in office, in the full & Just Sum of five hundred dollars, which payment well & truly to be made, we bind our Selves, heirs,

&C.

The Condition of the above Obligation is Such that, if the above Bound Sally Tindall

October Term 1818

Does in her own proper person be & appear at the Superior Court to held in & for Said County on the Second Monday in April Next, & not depart thence untill discharged by a due course of Law, than this Obligation to be Void, other wise to remain in full force & Virtue in Law. Given under our hands & Seals this 14th October 1818.

Maxfield H. Payne, Clk   Salah X Tindal, her mark
                                      Purnel Tindal
                                      Mathew Alexander

The State } vs } Assault & Battery
Benjamin Whitaker }
True Bill.   Sampson Laine, Foreman

The State   }
     vs   } Keeping open a tipling house on the Sabbath day
Michael Box }

True Bill.   Sampson Laine, Foreman

October Term 1818

John Hooper, app[t] }
     vs   } Trover
Willis Newton, Resp[t] }

Jury Sworn.

1. Sampson Lane   7. David Payne
2. Edward Carrell   8. John McIntire
3. Tho[s] Mayfield   9. Joseph Morris
4. James Tate   10. Gabriel Martin
5. Robert Hackett   11. Richard Gray   6. Joshua Hudson   12. Sam[l] Shannon

We, the Jury, find for the Defendant, with Cost of Suit.

                                      Sampson Lane, Forman

Joseph Yates }
     vs   } Trespass
David Crews }

Jury N° 2

We, the Jury, find for the plaintiff five dollars, with Cost of Suit. October 14th 1818

John M. Smith. Fm

The State }
    vs   } Misdemeanor
Walter Adair }
Edward Adair }
Samuel Ward }
Charles Ward }
James Hilton & }
Wm England }

True Bill.   Sampson Lane, fore^m

October Term 1818

Georgia }
Franklin County } The Grand Jury for the County afforesaid are truly Sorry that Circumstances, which we feel not at Liberty to disregard, has made it (as we conceive) our duty to notice as a Grievance the loose and ungarded manner in which the Inferior Court of this County has acted, as respects taking insufficient bail in the Case of the State against Noah Smith for Burglary.

We present Lewis Jones, John McMilbon, and Samuel H. Everett for Retailing Spirituous liquors without obtaining licens from the County.

We present Patsy Williams, otherwise called Patsey Holly for the crime of fornication. Witnesses Nathaniel Holley, Mary Holley, John Temples.

We present Michael Box, J^r for Suffering the evil and pernicious offence of Gambling in or on his premises.

We present John McMilbon for Keeping a tipling Shop open on the Sabbath and Suffering

October Term 1818

Five playing on the Same day. Witnesses Hudson Moss, William H. Wofford.

We present Dudley Jones for Suffering John Baird & John Bird to Gamble on his premises. Witnesses Maj^r Benjamin Cleveland, Job Hammond, and William Robins.

We present Joseph Murdock for living in a State of adultery, Suffering Gambling on his premises, and Keeping Open a tippling Shop on the Sabbath day. Witnesses Joseph J. Scott & William Robins.

We present John Bowman and Mary Cleveland for living in a State of a dultery. Witnesses Thos Wilkins, Jacob Cox.

We present Michael Box, J^r and Stephen Hopkins for Committing an affray on the night of the 12th instant in the Village of Carnesville. Abner Brown, witness.

October Term 1818

We present as a Grievance the General neglect of enforcing the patroll laws.

We feel gratified that we have in our power to present to his honor Judge Dooly our hearty thanks for his particular attention to the promotion of Virtue and morality So far as respects the functions of his office. Also for his unremitted diligence in Attening to County business during the present term.

    Sampson Lane, F. M.   Joshua Hudson
    Henrey Smith   Gabriel Martin
    Richd Gray   Ben^j Cleveland
    James Tait   Thomas Mayfield
    Robert Hackett   James Martin
    Garrett L. Sandidge   Samuel Shannon
    Hugh B. Greenwood   Maj^r Ben^j Cleveland
    David Payne   Edward Carrell
    Joseph Morris   Richd Allen
    John McEntire   John Wammack

Ex^d   Jn° M. Dooly

The Court then adjourned untill to morrow nine O'Clock.

Maxfield H. Payne, Clk

October Term 1818

The Court met according to adjournment 15th October 1818. Present, his honor Judge Dooly.

Maxfield H. Payne, Clk

Pettit Jury N° 1
    1. Nathl Williams   7. Aaron Sanders
    2. James Defur   8. Robert Crump
    3. Jeremaih Taylor   9. John Halcom
    4. Joseph Dobins   10. Robert Walters
    5. Saml Mackie   11. James Merrell
    6. Burrell Whitehead   12. Drury Rose

John Garner   }
     vs   } Trover & conversion
Dudley Jones }

Jury N° 1

We, the Jury, find for the Defendant, with Costs of Suit.

Burrell Whithead, F. M.

Moses Presley, for the }
of Wm U. Brown }
    vs   } assumpsit
John Denman & }
Richd Hutcherson }
Jury N° 1

We, the Jury, find for the plaintiff forty two dollars and thirty five Cents, with Interest and Cost of Suit.

Samuel Mackie, F. M.

October Term 1818

John Garner   }
   vs   } Trover &C
Dudley Jones } Judgment for Defendant

The Plaintiff, being dissatisfied with the above Verdict, came into Court and paid up the Cost & prayed an appeal, and at the Same time came John C. Aderhold with him and acknowledged himself Jointly & Severally bound Unto the Defendant for the eventual Condemnation money & Cost.

Witness our hands & Seals this 15th day of October 1818.

Maxfield H. Payne, Clk   John Garner, John C. Aderhold

Charles Sisson }
   vs   } Attach^t
Saml T. Cherry }

Jury N° 1

We find for the defendant.

Samuel Mackie, F. M.

The State } vs } Assault
Benjamin Whitaker }

Jury N° 1

We, the Jury, find the traverser guilty.

Samuel Mackie, F. M.

October Term 1818

The State }
vs } Ind^t Larceny from the Person
John Reed } Verdict Guilty

You, John Reed, are to be taken from the Bar of this Court to the Common Jail of the County, where you are to remain in Safe Custody until Saturday the Seventeenth day of this Instant October, on which Said 17th day of October, you are to be taken from said Jail by the proper officer and carried to the Penitentiary edifice of this of this State in the town of Milledgeville, and the Keeper of the Said Penitentiary is requested you, the said John Reed, into his Custody to take and receive and there Keep you in imprisonment in Said Penitentiary at hard labour for & during the term of five years, to be computed from the day of your Said Commitment to Said Penitentiary.

The State } vs
} Inti^{ct} Affray
Stephen Hopkins }

Know all men by these presents that I, Stephen Hopkins, am held and bound unto William Raburn, Govenor of said State, or his Successors in office, in the full sum of fifty dollars.

The condition of the above obligation is this, that if the said Stephen Hopkins do Appear at April Term of the Supr Court next and abide the order of said Court in the above stated case, then the obligation to be void, otherwise to remain in force in Law.

Given under my hand & seal in open Court 15th October 1818.

Maxfield H. Payne, Clk   Stephen Hopkins

The State } vs } Assault
Benjamin Whitaker }

to pay a fine of twenty five dollars & Cost of this prosecution & then be discharged.

Charles Sisson }
vs } Attach^t & Verdict for Defendant
Samuel T. Cherry }

The ~~Defendant~~ Plaintiff, being dissatisfied with the above Verdict, came into Court and paid up the Cost & prayed an appeal, and at the same time came John E. Carson with him and acknowledged himself Jointly and Severally Bound to the Defendant for the eventual condemnation money & Cost. In Witness Whereof, we have hereunto Set our hands & Seals this 15th October 1818.

Charles Sisson, Jn° E. Carson

Obadiah Neal }
    vs   } Certiorari
William Cain }

Sustained, proceedings below Set aside & a new trial order.

Thos Davis, Jr }
    vs   } Certiorari
James Menyard }

Sustained, proceedings below Set aside & a new trial ordered.

Lemuel G. MacMillin, Agent   }
& attorney in fact for Willis, Banks & C° }
vs }
Nathaniel Wofford   }

Dismissed.

Grand Jury Drawn for April Term 1819

1. Neely Dobson
2. Thompson Moore
3. Benjamin Cleveland, S. C.
4. John Mays
5. James Allan, Esqr
6. John Neal
7. Robert Hackett
8. James Jones, H. R.
9. James Gilbert
10. John McIntire
11. Thos F. Anderson
12. Samuel Headen
13. James Blair
14. James Tate
15. Lowry Gillaspie
16. David Henslee
17. Hamilton Winn
18. Robert Barnwell
19. Wm Bush
20. Benjn Starrett
21. Wm Gober, Son of Jon
22. Freeman Hardy, Ser
23. Benjn Cleveland, Capt
24. Samuel Yeargan
25. Robert Malone
26. Thos Lenoir
27. Francis Callaway, Jr
28. Joshua Hudson
29. Richd Gray
30. John Sandige
31. John E. Carson
32. Samuel Payne
33.
34.
35.
36.

James Hargrave & his wife }
Elizabeth Hargraves, in } right of the
said } Elizabeth Hargraves, }
Georeg W. Hudson & his wife }
Patsey Rosannah Hudson, in right } of
the said Patsey Rosannah &C }
  vs   } Bill for Discovery & Specific
Samuel Mackie & William Mackie } performance &C

Georgia, Franklin County Superior Court October Term 1818, on motion of Stephen Upson, Solicitor for complainant. It is ordered, that the Defendants plead, answer, or Demur, not Demuring alone, on or before the Second day of the next term of the Said Court, or the bill then to be taken pro confesso.

Pettit Jury Drawn for April Term 1819

1. Wm Clark
2. Thos Higgins
3. Isaiah Goolsby
4. Abel Mathews
5. David Crider
6. John Higgins
7. Sandford Higgins
8. Thos Ramsey
9. Jesse Brawner
10. Lewis Redwine
11. Green Chandler
12. Armsted Dowdy
13. Baker Ayers
14. James Higgins
15. Henry Brewer
16. John D. Hall
17. Ge^o Garner
18. Joel Moore
19. James Vessell
20. Ephram Vessell
21. Jesse Smith
22. Drury Jones
23. Wm Andrews
24. Enoch Andrews
25. Robert Williams
26. Armsted Murphy
27. John Hollingsworth
28. Asa Bradly
29. Wm Jackson
30. Victor Smith
31. Denniss Philips
32. James Manyard
33. Roland Wardon
34. Isham McBee
35. Jacob Campbell
36. James Stonecypher
37. Edwd Ryly
38. Wm Mays
39. Stephen Kirk
40. Elijah Crawford
41. Charles Jones
42. James Miller
43. David Miller
44. John Isom
45. Patterson Dodd
46. Ja^s Williams
47. Joel Thomas
48. Samuel White
49. Ephram Crain
50. Thos Baugers

Jane Cook, by her next } friend,
Ruseel Jones, Senr }
vs } Libel for Divorce Benjamin Cook }

Franklin Superior Court October Term 1818

In this Case, it appearing to the Court, that the Defendant is not to be found in the County; it is ordered, that the Said Benjamin do appear at the next Superior Court of Said County, as in default the Court will proceed in Said Case, and it is further ordered, that this order be published in One of the Gazettes of this State once a month for three months antecedent to the Sitting of Said Court.

Georgia County of Franklin Superior Court Octr Term 1818, the State by Samuel Commander, Prosecutor vs John Martin

On motion of Stephen Upson, attorney for John Martin, it is ordered, that he be discharged from his recognizance in this Case, & that the bond be Discharged as against him & his Securities.

The Court Then adjourned untill Court in Course.

Maxfield H. Payne, Clk

Ex^d Jno M. Dooly

Robert Mitchell }
vs } Trespass vi et armis & Verdict John Trigg }

Robert Mitchell }
vs } Trespass vi et armis & Verdict for the Plaintiff in both Cases John Trigg }

The Defendant, being dissatisfied with the above Verdicts, Came into Office and paid up the Cost & prayed an appeal in both Cases, and at the Same time Came Stephen Dickson with him and acknowledged himself Jointly and Severally bound unto the Plaintiff for the eventual Condemnation money & Costs.

In Witness whereof, we have hereunto Set our hands & Seals this 17th October 1818.

Maxfield H. Payne, Clk   John Trigg, Stephen Dickson

Moses Presley, for the } use
of Wm W. Bowen }
    vs   } Assumpsit & Verdict for plff
Richard Hutcherson }

The Defendant, Richard Hutcherson, came into Office. Paid up the Cost, & prayed a Stay of Execution Sixty days, and at the Same time Came Hezekiah Terrell, his

Security, & acknowledge himself bound with the Defendant to the plaintiff for the amount of the Judgment & Interest.

Witness our hands & Seals this 19th Octr 1818.

[blank], [blank]

Index

   Bob, 18, 19
   Daniel, 14
   David, 66
   George, 18, 19
   Wm., Sr., 42
Aaron
   William, 112
   Wm., 138
Adair
   Edward, 153
   Walter, 153
Adams
   Edward, 14
   Wm., 81
Aderhold
   John C., 156
Adrian
   John, 119
Adrine
   Benja., 40
   Fleming, 40
   Fleming F., 95
   Foweler F., 74, 78
Agee
   Humphey, 131
   Humphrey, 149
Aldine
   Arthur, 133
Alexander
   Arthur, 76
   M., 133
   Martha, 133, 152
   Mathew, 111, 133, 152
   Robert, 111
Allan
   Asa, 113
   James, 16, 19, 22, 24, 27, 30, 74, 105, 111, 113, 114, 117, 118, 120, 123, 158
   Jas., 22
   Richd., 16
Allbritton
   Isaac, 58, 121, 141
   Jno., 121
   John, 141
Allen
   Asa, 4, 12, 16, 74, 78, 84, 100, 106, 112, 113, 120, 123
   James, 100, 116
   John, Jr., 58
   Richard, 132, 144
   Richd., 74, 100, 141, 155
   Washington, 5, 101, 126, 132
Allexander
   Martha, 152
Allison
   David, 4, 31
Alston
   Lemuel J., 30
Anders
   Owen, 46
Anderson
   Livsey, 119
   Thomas, 52, 75
   Thomas F., 51, 52, 53
   Thos., 43, 58, 62, 66, 72, 85, 119
   Thos. F., 47, 158
Andrews
   Adam, 101
   Enoch, 159
   Enock, 86
   Owen, 43, 56
   Wm., 159

Anthoney
　David, 106, 107, 112, 117
Anthony
　David, 31, 101
　John, 5, 74
Armstrong
　James, 32, 92
　Jas., 86
　William, 96
Ash
　Alexander F., 134
　Alexr. F., 90, 91, 134
　Alx. F., 85
　John, 32
　William, 24, 32
　William, Sr., 4, 8
　Wm., Jr., 85
　Wm., Sr., 16, 142

Ashworth
  Benjamin, 120
  Elisha, 43
Askew
  John, 42
  Thos., 101
Avery
  Henry, 32, 34, 35, 36, 38, 86, 87, 91
Ayers
  Asa, 151
  Baker, 44, 85, 89, 159
  Baker, Jr., 44
  Garland, 44
  John, 5, 32, 34, 35, 119
  Ob., 42
  Obediah, 46, 47, 56
  William, 44
  Wm., 44
Bagley
  James, 123
Bagwell
  Matilda, 129, 132
  W. F., 26, 132 Winkd., 31
  Winkfield, 6, 23, 30, 129
Baird
  John, 149, 154
Baker
  ___, 86
  Absalom, 46, 56
  Beall, 32
  Benjamin, 141
  Benjn., Sr., 5
  Charles, 74, 80, 87
  Chris, 42, 100
  Christopher, 15, 46, 49, 50, 98, 117, 119, 124
  Christopher, Jr., 124
  Christopher, Sr., 131, 140
  Elias, 4, 8, 16, 130
  Green, 15, 95
  Greenberry, 113, 124
  Greenbery, 95
  James, 130
  John, 42, 46, 47, 56
  Joseph, 130
  William, 83
  Wm., 47
  Wm., Jr., 120
Baldwin
  Thomas, 70
  Thos., 62, 64
Ballenger
  David, 50
  Peter C., 92
Balwin
  Thos., 58
Bangs
  Jonathan, 58
Banks, 126, 158
  Ralph, 26, 139
  Willis, 140
Banneville
  Robt., 16
Barber
  Jno., 101
Barger
  George, 43
Barges
  Elias, 118
Bargey
  John, 59

Barna, 90, 96, 132
Barnett
  David, 110
  John F., 63
Barnhill
  Robert, 19, 30, 79, 89, 125, 129, 134, 137
  Robt., 27
  Wm., 85
Barns
  Robert, 74, 119, 125, 132
Barnwell
  Robert, 26, 119, 158
  Robt., 85
Barr
  Joseph, 90
Barratt
  Isaac J., 59
Barrett
  Isaac J., 16, 21, 39, 42, 45, 46, 70, 96, 100, 118
Barrons
  Henry, 4, 9
Barton
  Hutchins, 17
  Jno., 86
  John, 31, 58, 62, 64, 92, 96, 97
Bask
  John, 16
Baugers
  Thos., 159
Baugh
  John, 27, 31, 34, 41, 130
  Jonathan, 32, 63, 114, 115, 117, 126
  Mary, 117

Baxter
  Reuben, 74, 78, 83, 87
Beach, 93, 109
Beall
  Daniel, 75, 132
  F., 21, 25, 26, 32, 77, 126, 129,
    130, 131, 137, 138
  Freadrick, 14
  Fred, 133
  Frederick, 18, 19, 125, 129, 137,
  143
  Fredk., 16, 18, 24, 25, 26, 33, 74, 119, 126, 134, 136, 138, 139,
  143
  Wm., 94
Bealls
  Frederick, 95
Beasley
  John, 116, 119
Beazley
  John, 125, 127, 129, 135, 138
Becham
  Benj., 142
Beck, 59
  John, 59, 149
Bellamy
  John, 4, 9, 10, 58, 63, 69, 71, 151
Bennett
  Hardiman, 92
Bevan
  Joseph, 9, 10, 18, 19
Bevins
  Robet, 85

Bird
  John, 149, 154
Black
  William, 90
Blackbourn
  Wm. A., 109
  Blackburn
  Ambrose, 20 Ambrous, 39
  William A., 15, 70, 79, 83
  Wm. A., 25, 31, 82, 83, 93
Blackwell
  Jesse, 32, 58, 62, 64, 71
  Wm., 43, 46, 47, 56
Blag
  Israel, 56
Blagg
  Daniel, 56
  Israel, 8, 9, 23, 25
Blair
  James, 16, 19, 88, 97, 119, 158
  Thomas, 17
  Thos., 142
  Wm., 120
  Bleur
  James, 42
Bobo
  Lewis, 26
  Sampson, 5, 14
Bole
  William, 31, 34, 35, 39
  Wm., 44
Boling
  William, 51
Bollenger
  David, 49
Bond
  Nathan, 119, 125, 127, 129, 135,
    138
  Richard, Sr., 34, 35, 39
  Richd., 17
  Richd., Jr., 59
  Richd., Sr., 31
  Robt., 59
Bonds
  Robt., 17
Boon
  Martin, 51
Boroughs
  Henry, 86
Bowen
  Wm. W., 160
Bowman
  John, 32, 34, 35, 62, 74, 141, 151, 154
  Winnifred, 62
Box
  Jonathan, 114, 128
  M___, 80
  Michael, 153
  Michael, Jr., 123, 142, 154
  Michael, Sr., 74
Bracher
  Amos, 29
Bradberry
  Salathiah, 11
Bradbury
  Salathiah, 13
Bradly
  Asa, 159
Brady
  Enoch, 17, 108, 112, 117
  Enock, 101

Bramblett
  Reuben, 42
Branch
  Harris, 74
  Braswell
  Fredk., 42
Braszel
  Fredk., 47
Braszell
  Frederick, 56
  Fredk., 46
Bratcher
  A., 22, 29, 30
  Amos, 28, 75, 103, 132
  Nancy, 28
Bratchers
  Amos, 28
Brather
  Amos, 6, 148
Brawner
  Jesse, 32, 34, 35, 86, 89, 159
Bray
  Thomas, 7
Brazer
  Saml., 43
Brewer
  Henry, 91, 159
Brice, 122
  John, 47, 50
Bridges
  Jno., 97
  John, 97
Brien
  Robert, 37
Bright
  Saml., 127

Samuel, 129
Brogdon
  David, 138
  Sally, 138
Brooks
  Job, 101
Brown
  Abner, 154
  Isaac, 104, 120
  James, 97, 104, 105, 120
  James N., 139
  Jno., Sr., 85
  John, 32, 119, 131, 135
  John R., 4, 5, 6, 7, 9, 10, 12,
    13, 14, 15, 18, 19, 26, 42,
    46, 50, 55, 56, 59, 61, 63,
    65, 70, 99,
    120, 135
  John, Jr., 91
  Meredith, 19, 22, 27, 30, 42,
    46,
    59
  Peter, 17, 20, 24, 29, 59, 150
  Peters, 63
  Richard, 120
  Rigdon, 78
  Robert, 135
  William, 127
  Wm., 70, 119
  Wm. U., 155
  Wyatt, 34
Bruce
  Robert, 58, 62, 66, 69, 71, 72,
    75, 105, 118, 120, 123,
    141, 146
  Robt., 100
Bruice

Robert, 113, 144
Brumley
  Stephen, 98, 116, 118
Bryan
  Edward, 65
  Eli, 50, 65, 87, 99, 120
  John, 108, 109, 110, 139
  John, Jr., 120
  Royal, 85, 89, 96, 99, 102, 121
  Wm. B., 111 Bryce, 87, 104
Burges
  Elias, 69, 74, 78, 84, 106
Burgess
  Elias, 100, 123
Burk
  Wm., 46
Burns
  Robert, 128
Buroughs
  Thos. P., 110
Burroughs
  Henry, 92
Burt
  William, 83
Burton
  John, 71
  Robert, 126, 134
  Robt., 134
  Saml., 32, 74
  Samuel, 78, 82, 87
Bush, 48, 108
  John, 4, 31, 58, 62, 73, 75, 85, 115
  William, 27, 48, 59
  Wm., 42, 119, 158
Byford

Aquilla, 64
Cail
  James, 17
Cain
  James B., 111
  William, 157
Cairrell
  George, 9
Callaway
  Francis, 63
  Francis, Jr., 158
Camp
  Abisha, 80, 113, 118, 120
Campbell, 137
  Aaron, 16, 42
  D. G., 124, 133, 137
  Duncan G., 12, 19, 54, 124
  J. W., 54, 55
  Jacob, 159
  John, 43, 46, 47, 56
  John W., 54, 55
  John Warlty, 54
Camron
  Absalom, 90
Cannon
  Henry, 142
Carnes
  Holloway, 111
  Jno. P., 142
  John P., 82, 93
  Richd., 111
  T. H. P., 6
  Thos., 47
  Thos. P., 60
  Wells, 111
Carns

   Richd., 42
   Thomas, 43
Carpenter
   George, 58
   Temple, 63
Carrell
   ___, 85
   Clement, 63, 69
   Clemment, 71
   Clemt., 58
   Edward, 62, 66, 72, 75, 144, 148, 150, 151, 153, 155
   Edward D., 58
   Edwd., 141
   Geo., 142
   George, 4, 10, 83
   John, 74, 80
Carson
   Jno. E., 157
   John E., 31, 34, 35, 36, 39, 41, 74, 77, 78, 79, 84, 109, 112, 116, 119, 125, 133, 157, 158
Carter, 57, 60
   Charles, 44
   Jarrat, 57
   Jarratt, 60, 61
   Thomas, 44
   Thomas S., 44
   Thos., 58, 63, 69, 71
Caruth
   William, 43
Cary
   James, 134
Cawthen
   Charles, 74
Cawthon

   Charles, 78, 79, 80, 81, 87
   Chesley, 32, 34, 35, 119
   Larkin, 25
   Rhoda, 29, 33
   William, 25, 33, 102, 121, 125, 141
   Wm., 29, 85, 89, 99, 119, 129, 134, 137
Chalmers
   John, 82
Chambers
   Wm., 145
Chandler
   Allen, 43, 47, 120
   Green, 95, 113, 124, 159
   Janes, 35
   John, 92, 98
   Joseph, 26, 31, 34, 36, 41, 46, 47, 58, 62, 66, 72, 74, 75, 78, 84, 85, 89, 91, 102, 105, 108, 112, 119, 125, 129, 133, 137, 142, 143
   Richard, 91, 92, 105, 133, 143
   Robert, 35, 147, 151
   Robt., 142
   Starling, 84
   Sterling, 74, 78
   Wm., 92
   Zach, 142
   Zachariah, 82, 147
Chatham
   Chafin, 74
   Epps, 42
   Stephen, 101

William, 106
Wm., 101, 106, 107, 112, 117
Cherry
　Elijah, 129
　Saml. T., 156
　Samuel T., 157
Chisolm
　William, 17, 29
　Wm., 33
Christian
　Elijah, 92
　Presley, 107, 121, 125
Cimmins
　Eliz, 54
　Elizabeth, 64
　Robert, 8, 64
Cimmons
　Robert, 54
Clark
　John, 82
　Thomas, 49, 70
　Thos., 16, 43, 46, 47, 56, 62, 64
　Thos., Jr., 58
　William, 108, 110, 116
　Wm., 159
Clarkson
　John, 16, 20, 22, 24, 59, 62, 64
Clement
　Adam, 126, 145
Cleveland
　Absalom, 63, 93
　Ben, 100
　Benj., 155
　Benja., 31, 32, 35, 70, 78, 85
　Benjamin, 15, 70, 84, 144, 154, 158

Benjn., 4, 13, 74, 141, 142, 148, 158
John, 57, 61, 116, 133
Larkin, 55, 99
Mary, 154
William, 60
Wyat, 85
Wyatt, 58, 74, 119
Cloud
　Adam, 26, 66, 72, 76, 81, 86, 101
　Jno. W., 72
　John W., 66, 81, 86, 101
Coats
　Janus, 64
Cobb
　Thomas W., 87
　Thos. W., 104
Cockburn
　Archabald, 20, 23
　Archabld, 142
　Archibald, 17
　George, 31
Cockerban
　Peter, 80
Cogburn
　Archabald, 24
　Archd., 29
Coil
　John, 32
Coker
　Thomas, 68
Collier
　H___, Jr., 119
Collins
　Andrew, 98

Commander
  Samuel, 160
Commins
  Robt., 22
Compty
  John R., 130
Conn
  Thos., 119, 125, 129, 135, 138
Connally
  David, 92
Conner
  Boley, 63, 65, 74, 78, 84, 87, 98, 99, 108, 120, 135
  John, 74
Cook, 6, 118
  Benjamin, 159
  Elisha, 58, 63, 69, 70
  Geo., 6, 54
  Jane, 159
  Joseph, 49, 67
Cooper, 106
  Benjamin, 92, 106
Corkerham
  Peter, 74
Cornelius
  Absalom, 59
Cowden
  John, 63
Cox
  Aries, 27
  Aris, 5, 42, 47
  Jacob, 126, 154
  John, 128
  Mathew, 12
  Robt. R., 86
  Thomas, 31, 103, 121
  Thos., 47, 103, 142
Crain
  Ephram, 159
Crawford
  Elijah, 159
  Hugh, 107
Crenshaw
  William, 101
  Wm., 66, 72, 81, 86
Crews
  David, 153
Crider
  David, 86, 159
Crump
  John, 32, 34, 35, 101
  Robert, 144, 147, 151, 155
  Robt., 142
  Silas, 139
Cunningham
  John, 64
Dabbs
  Richard, 110
Dabs
  Jesse, 142
Dailey
  Saml., 74, 78
Daily
  Samuel, 87
David
  Jesse, 6
Davidson
  Hugh, 58, 100, 105, 118, 120, 123, 141
Davis
  Henry, 101, 108, 111, 112, 117
  Nancy, 60, 66

Thomas, 78
Thomas W., 87, 123, 149
Thos., Jr., 74, 100, 158
Van, 48
William, 60, 66 Wm. H., 149
Davison
  Richd., 86
Dawdy
  Jas., 100
Defeur
  James, 142
Defur
  James, 147, 151, 155
Defurr
  James, 144
Denman
  Chris, 100
  Christopher, 48, 106, 107, 112, 114, 117
  James, 135, 138, 141
  Jno., 101
  John, 108, 133, 155
Denmore
  James, 31
Diar
  Elisha, 142
Dickerson
  Jos., 85
  Joseph, 91, 97
Dickson
  Stephen, 114, 143, 160
Dilbert
  John, 53
Dixon
  Stephen, 59, 72, 143
Dobbins
  Joseph, 17, 144, 147, 151
Dobbs
  Jeremiah, 69
  Jesse, 71
  John, 55
  Peter, 55, 69
Dobins
  Jos., 142
  Joseph, 155
Dobson, 96
  N., 96, 102
  Neely, 31, 34, 41, 58, 61, 66, 85, 89, 96, 99, 141, 158
Dodd
  Patterson, 159
Doe, 20
  John, 6, 7, 21, 35, 48, 88, 94, 109, 111, 117, 125
Dooly, 6, 57, 60, 89, 93, 97, 100, 105, 112, 117, 121, 123, 125, 139, 143, 147, 154, 155
  Jno. M., 93, 97, 100, 105, 112, 115, 117, 121, 124, 128, 131, 134, 140, 143, 146, 150, 155, 160
Dorsey
  Benja., 26, 42
  Benjamin, 13, 18, 21, 33, 82, 95, 104, 135
  Benjn., 16, 19, 93
  John, 17, 43, 46, 56
Dowdy
  Armsted, 159
Downs

John, 120
Dox, 95
Dunagan
  Abner, 106, 113, 118
Duncan
  John, 62, 73, 75, 85, 119, 125,
    129, 133, 137 John, Jr.,
  58
Dunnagan
  Abner, 118
Dunnagin
  Abner, 42, 100
Dunnigan
  Abner, 16, 22, 27, 30
Dunnigin
  Abner, 19
Dye
  Stephen, 76, 77
Dyer
  Wiley, 110
Early
  Edward, 68
  Peter, 67
Earwood
  Andrew, 142
Echols
  Darias, 74
  Darius, 141, 145
  John, 120
Eddins
  William, 20, 83
  Wm., 17, 22, 24, 29, 74, 80, 82
Edward
  James W., 126, 149
  Joseph, 58
Edwards
  Ed, 100

James W., 149
Joseph, 34, 39, 41, 43, 63, 67, 68,
  69, 70
Wm., 142
Elliott
  Wm., 104
Ellison
  David, 5
Embry
  Joseph, 27
England
  Charles, 16
  James, 153
English
  John, 56, 88
Epperson
  John, 130
  Thompson, 4, 13, 15, 77
Everett
  John, 9, 23, 25, 56
  Saml. H., 4, 16, 58, 100, 106,
  113
  Samuel H., 123, 154
Eveverett, 56
Fagan
  Philip, 114, 115
Farmer
  Thos., 120
Ferguson
  Saml., 42
Findley
  Kinneth, 69, 71
Finley
  Kinneth, 85
Flannagin
  Wm., 101

Fleming
  Elijah, 111 James, 123
  Moses, 47
  Robert, 34, 35, 39
  Robt., 31, 142
  Wm., 142, 147
Flood
  James, 43
Foote
  William, 144
Ford
  David, 42
  Ricd., 85
Foreman
  Winsette, 16
Freeman
  John W., 145
Friar
  Isaac, 64
Fullerton
  Robert, 50
Ganes
  Larch, 142
Garner
  Geo., 159
  Jacob, 32
  John, 155, 156
Garrison
  Caleb, 82, 87
  Christopher, 74
  Levi, 34, 41
  Thomas, 91
  Thos., 86
  Zebulon, 93, 94, 95, 114, 120
Garrisson
  Calob, 74, 80, 82

John, 16, 19, 58
Levi, 31
Levy, 74
Gasaway
  John, 119
Gazoway
  Thomas, 43
Gest
  Moses, 100
  Wm., 101
Gilbert
  James, 123, 158
  John, 64, 65
  Thomas, 128
Gillaspie
  Lowry, 58, 61, 62, 75, 100, 119,
    125, 158
Gillespie
  Lowry, 132
Gilley
  Charles, 145
  John, 110
Gilmer, 137
  Geo. R., 137
Glascock
  James, 94
  Leroy, 94
Glenn
  Joseph, 27
  Nancy, 139
  Simson, 139
Gloland
  Saml., 141
Glover
  William, 47
  Wm., 42

Gober
  George, 32, 74, 80
  Jack, 16, 120
  Jas., 142
  John, 16, 29
  Thomas, 17
  Thos., 22, 101, 106, 112, 117
  Wm., 58, 62, 63, 64, 65, 66, 68, 158
Goodson
  Wm., 58
Goodwin
  William, 37, 122
Goolsby
  Isaiah, 159
  Thomas, 139 William, 139
  Wm., 139
Gorham
  John, 44
  Sandford, 90, 91, 93, 94, 96, 97, 98, 102
  Sanford, 85
  Thomas, 49
  Thos., 49, 103
Gray
  John M., 17
  R. D., 20, 21, 23, 26, 30
  Rd., 20
  Richard, 17, 22, 40, 59, 78, 144, 148, 153
  Richard D., 23
  Richd., 20, 46, 74, 141, 155, 158
  Richd. D., 29
  Rid D., 20
Greenwood
  Beverley, 109
  Beverly, 121, 124, 125, 148
  H. B., 66, 102, 141, 148
  Hugh B., 32, 58, 62, 75, 85, 89, 96, 144, 148, 150, 151, 155
Gresham, 4, 7, 8, 11, 17, 19, 21, 24, 32, 34, 35, 38, 40, 41, 45, 53, 58, 61, 65, 70, 72, 73, 75, 77, 79, 81, 82, 83, 85
  Young, 7, 8, 11, 16, 19, 21, 22, 23, 28, 32, 33, 35, 38, 40, 41, 45, 47, 53, 54, 57, 61, 64, 65, 67, 69, 72, 73, 77, 79, 81, 82, 85, 88
Griffin
  Cabot, 58
Griffith
  Caleb, 53, 85, 96, 105, 119
Grogg
  Thomas, 135
Grovor
  Peter, 81
Guest
  Calbert, 108
  Moses, 58, 62, 105, 118, 120
  Moses, Jr., 75
Hacket
  Robert, 58
Hackett
  Robert, 16, 17, 47, 60, 85, 89, 96, 99, 102, 116, 135, 142, 144, 148, 150, 151, 153, 155, 158

William, 4, 8, 13, 31, 125
Wm., 16, 34, 35, 41, 74, 78, 84,
   92, 119, 129, 133, 134
Haden
   Saml., 74
   Samuel, 22, 123
Haiden
   Samuel, 27
Halcom
   John, 151, 155
Halcomb
   Jno., 142
   John, 82
   Richd., 16, 142
Haley
   James, 63, 74, 80 James R., 116
Hall
   Elijah, 17
   John D., 159
   Sarah, 9
   William H., 37
Hamilton
   Andrew, 9, 13
   Joseph, 33, 51, 76, 120 Polley, 76, 120
Hammond
   Job, 154
Hanna
   James, 104
Hansford
   Jesse B., 85
Harbaun
   Halman, 139
Harber
   John, 58, 62, 69
Harboin
   Esaias, 31

Harbor
   Thomas, 91
   Thos., 86
Harden
   Richard, 126
   Sawan, 19
   Swan, 11, 13, 22
Hardin
   Richard, 145
   Swan, 16
Hardon
   Richd., 74
Hardy
   Freeman, 58, 85, 158
Hargrave
   James, 23, 158
Hargraves
   Elizabeth, 158
Hargrove
   James, 4, 23, 58
   Jas., 10, 11
Hargroves
   James, 9, 10, 12, 38
   Jas., 5, 7
Harmon
   John, 131
Harnes
   T. H., 54
Harrington
   Stephen, 16
   Thomas, 83
Harris, 6, 54
   Absalom, 146
   Bradock, 52
   Jeptha V., 49, 69
   Sterling, 63

Walton, 14, 27, 54, 76, 104
Harrison
  ___ Y., 16
  Richard, 39
  Robert, 20, 29
  Robt., 58
  Spencer, 101
Harrisson
  Robert, 22, 24, 65
Haynes
  John, 27
  Moses, 145
  Sarah, 27
Haynie
  George, 78, 88, 147
Headen
  Saml., 85, 89, 102, 132, 133
  Samuel, 19, 119, 125, 137, 158
Heard
  John A., 140
Hearden
  Saml., 16
Hearndon
  William, 91, 126
Hedden
  Samuel, 129
Henderson
  James, 32, 34, 120
Henley, 108
  Darby, 16, 19, 22, 27, 108, 119, 125, 133
  Edmd., 42
  Edmond, 38
  Edmund, 4, 8, 12, 13, 14, 44, 46, 89, 96, 99, 102, 105, 108, 112, 113
  Jane, 12, 38
  Mary, 12, 38
  William, 12, 38
Henly
  Darby, 27, 85
  Edmond, 16
  Edmund, 59, 85
Henslee
  David, 158
Herndin
  Martin, 31
Herring
  Moses, 21
Hifield
  Benjamin, 8
  Benjn., 4
Higgin
  Reuben, 121
Higgins
  James, 159
  John, 159
  Sandford, 159
  Thos., 159
Highfield
  Benjn., 101
Hightower
  William, 97
Hill
  John, 27
  Thomas, 32, 34, 35, 90, 96
  Thos., 86
Hilton
  James, 153
Hobson
  James, 39
  Sarah, 39
Hogwood

Wyly, 74, 80
Holbrook
  Edy, 117
  Jesse, 59, 108
  John, 101, 106, 112, 117
  William, 46, 47, 138
  Wm., 56, 119, 125, 127, 129, 135
Holbrooks
  William, 43
Holcom
  Absalom, 76
  John, 74, 83, 147, 151
Holcomb
  John, 144
Holingsworth
Jas., 142
Holland
  James, 64
  Jesse, Jr., 42
  Labon, 64
  Sarah, 65
  Wm., 58
Holley, 130
  Frederick, 80, 82
  Fredk., 74
  Mary, 154
  Nathaniel, 154
  Pleasant, 74 William, 19
  Wm., 16
Hollingsworth
  Henry, 73
  J., 90, 96, 132
  Jacob, 60, 73, 77
  Jacob J., 73
  James, 4, 59
  John, 27, 159

Saml., 27, 59, 60, 77
Samuel, 73
Thomas, 59, 96, 97, 123, 132
Thos., 16, 19, 42, 46, 90, 97, 100,
  105, 118, 141
Holly
  Patsy, 154
Holt
  Larkin, 86
Hoop
  John, 102
Hooper
  James, 4, 13, 15, 42, 46, 89, 112,
    113, 119
  James, Jr., 88
  John, 4, 8, 13, 16, 52, 59, 76, 85,
    89, 96, 99, 139, 153
  John W., 136, 137
  Joshua, 5, 98, 103
  Richard, 4, 8, 15, 17, 75, 85
  Richd., 58, 62
  William, 52, 78
  Wm., 10, 78
Hopkins
  Stephen, 154, 157
Horn
  Jesse, 94
Howington
  Wilson, 43
Hudson
  George W., 158
  John, 16, 58
  Joshua, 4, 8, 13, 24, 31, 62, 75, 100, 105, 118, 120,

123, 141, 144, 148, 150, 151, 153, 155, 158
Patsey Rosannah, 158
Hulsey
  James, 39
  James, Sr., 42
  James. Sr., 46
  Wm., 58, 100, 119
Hunt
  Joel, 16, 20, 22, 24, 29, 86, 92
Hunter
  Nancy, 79
Hutcherson
  Richard, 85, 99, 102, 141, 160
  Richd., 58, 155
Hyde
  Thomas, 51
Irby
  William, 117, 126
Isam
  Charles, 32
Isham
  Edwd., 58
Ishaw
  Charles, 100
Isom
  John, 159
Ivey
  Thos., 16
Ivy
  John, 86, 87, 89, 94, 120
  Thomas, 46, 52, 70
  Thos., 142, 147, 151
Jackson
  James, 119
  Joseph, 136
  William, 136
  Wm., 136, 159
Jacobs
  Wm., 20
Jarrett
  Deveraux, 84
  Deveroux, 78, 119
  Devroux, 74
Jarrott
  Deveroux, 17
Jay
  Thom, 66
Jenkins
  John, 16
Jewell
  Greenberry, 74
Johnston
  James, 101
  John, 80
Jones
  Charles, 159
  Drury, 159
  Dudley, 18, 21, 31, 33, 52, 58, 74, 87, 93, 95, 100, 101, 104, 111, 119, 122, 125, 132, 135, 154, 155, 156
  Jabez, 109, 121, 124, 148
  James, 43, 46, 47, 56, 158
  Joseph, 91
  Lewis, 154
  Martin, 91
  Peter, 120, 125, 127, 129, 135, 138
  Russell, 31
  Russell, Sr., 159

Thos., 74
Tignal, 58, 62, 64, 71
William, 19
Wm., 16, 22, 27, 42, 46, 59
Jordan
  Elias, 74, 80, 82, 116
  James, 32, 74
  T. D., 102
  Thomas D., 47
  Thos. D., 85, 89, 96, 99, 144
  Wm. H., 79, 86
Kendrick
  Austin, 42
Kilpatrick, 65
King, 48
  Benjamin, 59, 149
  Edmd., Jr., 74, 78, 84, 100
  Edmd., Sr., 42
  Edmund, 12, 38, 44, 48, 51, 60
  Edmund, Jr., 4, 8, 13, 15, 27, 59, 71, 119
  Edmund, Sr., 16, 46
  Elizabeth, 44, 51, 60
  George, 26, 47, 80, 82, 83
  Lambard, 87
  Lemberd, 74, 83
  Lembord, 78
Kirk
  Stephen, 144, 159
Kitchen
  Stephen, 18
Knox
  Joh. W., Jr., 114
  John, 123
  John, Jr., 110, 114, 145
Lacy

Jordan, 15
Laine
  Sampson, 148, 149, 150, 153
Lane
  Clyveland, 139
  Garland, 44
  Jno., 36
  John, 66
  John, Jr., 37
  Sampson, 31, 34, 36, 39, 41, 74, 78, 79, 84, 94, 106, 118, 123, 129, 132, 141, 144, 146, 147, 148, 149, 150, 151, 153, 155
  Samson, 100
  Spn., 84, 132, 151
Langfared
  Robert, Jr., 17
Langford
  Abner, 92
Langston
  Asa, 106, 115, 149
  James, 49
Lankford
  Abner, 92
  Wyatt, 142
Laurens
  Joel, 16
Lausone
  Joel, 59
Lawhon
  A., 71
  Allen, 136
Leach
  Asa, 5, 52, 58, 62, 64, 70
Leath

Wm., 101
Leathers
  Nancy, 64
  Nimrod, 64, 69, 70, 113
Leavell
  Edwd., 42
Legg
  William, 51, 130
Lendsey
  James, 100
Lenoir
  Mary, 59
  T., 102
  Thomas, 59, 73, 96
  Thos., 4, 9, 10, 85, 89, 99, 158
Lenorir
  Mary, 77
  Thomas, 77
Lewellen
  Joseph, 108
Liddle
  Moses, 85, 89, 96, 99
Little
  Green H., 16
  James H., 58, 61, 69, 71, 75, 85, 89, 98, 99, 102, 128
  Jas. H., 69, 92, 95, 98
  Moses, 102
Logan
  James, 18, 76
Loley
  William, 64
Long
  James, 18
Longmire
  George, 58, 108
Longmires
  George, 63, 69, 71
Love
  Benja., 32
  Benjamin, 75
  Benjn., 58, 62 Isaac, 74
Lovin
  Edmd., 86
Lowell
  James, 26
Lowerey
  Jas., Jr., 142
Lowrey
  James, 43
  Wm., 78
Lowry
  Benj., 120
  Benjamin, 135, 138
  Benjn., 125, 127, 129
  Christopher, 30
  David, 119
  Elisha, 101
  Eliz., 84
  Elizabeth, 80, 83
  Jas., Jr., 101
  John, 84, 85 William, 87
  Wm., 74, 82
Mabrey
  Pat, 101
Mabry
  Epham, 10
  Ephraim, 4, 9
  Patrick, 17
Mackee
  Samuel, 144
Mackie

Saml., 146, 155
Samuel, 145, 147, 151, 152, 156, 158
William, 158
MacMillin
  Lemuel G., 158
Malden
  Richard, 5, 27
Malone
  Robert, 4, 13, 27, 30, 158
Malonee
  Robert, 16
Malry
  Ephram, 74
Manly
  David B., 24
Mann
  Henry, 80
Manyard
  James, 159
Mareen
  James, 76
Markham
  Squire, 42, 46
Martin
  Bryan, 37
  Gabl., 100
  Gabriel, 42, 106, 113, 118, 120, 123, 141, 144, 148, 150, 151, 153, 155
  Gabril, 24
  James, 42, 59, 141, 155
  James, Sr., 46
  Jas., 100
  John, 58, 87, 160
  Jos., 62, 66
  Joseph, 31, 36, 37, 58, 62, 70, 73, 75, 142
  William, 9, 47, 83
  Wm., 83
Mathews, 26
  Abel, 159
  Charles L., 77
  George, 14
Maulders
  Richd., 27
Maxwell
  Thos., 74
  William, 64
Mayes
  John, 89, 96, 137
Mayfield
  John, 16, 19, 30, 113, 118, 144, 148, 150, 151
  John, Jr., 58, 100, 105, 123, 141
  Thomas, 84, 106, 118, 123, 144, 155
  Thos., 74, 78, 100, 113, 141, 148, 150, 151, 153
Maynard
  Edward, 17
Mays
  Jno., 102
  John, 80, 85, 101, 113, 117, 119, 125, 129, 134, 158
  Thomas, 24
  Thos., 101
  Wm., 159
McBee
  Isham, 17, 159
McCarter

James, 120
Mathew, 32, 34, 35, 58, 63, 64, 71
McCarty
  James, 24
McClain
  James, 74
McCormick
  David, 10
McCracken
  Wm., 32, 96
McDaid
  John, 5
McDaniel
  Chiswell, 25
McDonald
  James, 14, 42, 46, 80
McDow
  John, 7, 101, 106, 107, 108, 109, 110, 112, 113, 115, 117
McEntire
  John, 31, 62, 75, 155
McFarlin
  Robert, 101, 106, 107, 117
McGrady
  Arch, 43
  Jos., 86
McIntire
  James, 102
  Jno., 102
  John, 41, 66, 67, 73, 85, 89, 96, 99, 141, 144, 148, 150, 151, 153, 158
McIntyre
  John, 34, 35
McKee
  Saml., 142, 144
McKie
  Samuel, 12, 23, 24, 38, 39, 147
  William, 12, 23
  Wm., 38
McKinne, 87, 90, 96
McKinney, 132
  Wilson, 130
McMilbon
  John, 154
McNeal
  John, 35, 41
McNeel
  John, 31, 34
Meadows
  John, 32
Medcock
  Isham, 79
Meeks
  Littleton, 4, 8, 15, 42
Melton
  Robert, 70, 71
Menyard
  James, 158
Mercer
  James, 17, 20, 23, 24, 29, 120, 125, 127, 129, 138
  John, 101
Merrell
  James, 147, 151, 155
Miller
  David, 4, 9, 10, 86, 159
  James, 159
  John, 106
Milner
  Jeremiah, 43, 78, 88, 89, 110,

147
Milton
  Robert, 46
Milweed
  Wm., 122 Mise
  Zach, 142
Mitchel
  Robert, 147
Mitchell
  David, 32, 82, 119, 127, 144
  James, 24, 29, 47, 57, 74, 78
  Jas., 84
  Robert, 148, 160
  Wm., 120 Molder
  Lewis, 89
  Richard, 120
Montgomery Hugh, 14
Moor
  George W., 51
Moore
  Adam, 64
  Joel, 159
  Thompson, 42, 46, 59, 119, 125, 129, 133, 137, 158
  William, 64
Morgan
  David, 36, 86, 91
  Saml., 17, 74, 100
  Samuel, 93, 94, 95, 114
  Thomas, 32, 40, 70, 93, 94, 95, 114
  Thos., 58, 62, 64, 95
Morris, 141
  James, 123
  Jo, 119
  John, 31, 34, 36, 41

Joseph, 31, 34, 35, 41, 58, 62, 75, 100, 105, 113, 118, 120, 123, 141, 144, 148, 150, 151, 153, 155
Moss
  Barbara, 28
  Hudson, 44, 51, 53, 118, 154
Moulder
  Lewis, 77, 85, 128
Mullin
  Jno., 100, 136
  John,   57
  Thomas, Mullins   136
  John,   141
  Thomas,   163
  Joseph,   164
  Armsted,   171
Murdock
Murphy
Murray, 87, 104, 122
Nail
  John, 40, 42, 46, 59, 130
  Joseph, 130
Naylor
  Polydore, 88, 145
Neal
  Alexander, 97
  John, 4, 8, 48, 90, 103, 119, 125, 129, 133, 137, 140, 158
  Joseph, 129, 140
  Major, 39, 58, 63
  Obadiah, 157
  Robert, 46, 142
  Robt., 59

Thomas, 42
Neale
  Robert, 100
Neel
  Major, 31
  Robert, 42
  Thomas, 27
Nesbit
  Hugh, 13
Newton
  Thomas, 31
  Willis, 139, 153
Nickson
  John, 85
  Jos., 85
Nix
  James, 143
Nixon
  John, 89
  Joseph, 89
Nunn
  Thomas, 83, 94
  Thos., 5, 74
O'Kelly
  George W., 146
Odam
  John, 58
Oliver, 137
  James, 12, 137
Osbarn
  Ephraim B., 107
Osborn
  Ephraim, 131
Osburn
  Nelson, 80
Page
  Berry, 52
  William, 86, 89
  Wm., 94, 111
Paine, 13, 54, 137
  Edmund, 46
  Edward, 54, 137
  G. D., 47, 144
  Geo. Drury, 13
  George D., 14
  John, Sr., 35
  William, 29, 33
Palmer
  E., 124
  Edward, 112, 115, 124, 150
  Elizabeth, 124
Parks
  Henry, 24, 31, 34, 41
Parnell
  Absalom, 16
  Moses, 35
Patterson
  Tryon, 83
Paxon
  Lenor, 142
Payn
  Thos., Sr., 16
Payne, 68
  Charles, 5, 17, 33
  David, 58, 62, 100, 106, 113, 118, 141, 144, 148, 150, 151, 153, 155
  Hanslu, 110
  John, 40
  John, Jr., 120
  John, Sr., 31, 34, 41

Joseph, 27, 58, 62, 66, 75, 100, 105, 118, 141
M. H., 61
Maxfield H., 7, 8, 11, 16, 19, 21, 22, 23, 26, 28, 32, 33, 35, 38, 40, 41, 42, 45, 46, 53, 55, 58, 64, 65, 69, 70, 72, 73, 77, 79, 81, 82, 85, 88, 89, 93, 95, 97, 100, 103, 105, 112, 114, 115, 116, 117, 121, 124, 125, 128, 131, 132, 134, 135, 136, 137, 140, 143, 146,147, 150, 152, 155, 156, 160
Nathaniel, 68
Reuben, 5, 52, 85, 89, 141
Saml., 85, 89, 96, 102
Samuel, 96, 99, 119, 158
Sarah, 26
Thomas, 26, 36
Thos., 19, 30, 85

Peak
  Abel, 5
Pearce
  John, 85
Pearson
  John, 89
  John, Jr., 55
Perdu
  Larkin, 116
Perry
  Benjn., 63
Presley
  Moses, 155, 160
Prewett John T., 91 Saml., 71
Prewit
  Ben, 101
Prewitt

Petitford
  Nathan, 74
Philips
  Cleverly, 23
  Clevery, 86
  Denniss, 159
Phillips
  Cleverly, 6, 92
  Dennis, 81
  Samuel, 12, 38
Pitchford
  Nathan, 78, 87
Plaster
  Benjamin, 108, 114, 127, 135, 138
  Benjn., 119, 125, 129
Poe
  Stephen, 4, 8, 16, 42, 46
Pool
  Wm., 74, 78, 119
Poole
  Wm., 84
Pope, 59
  Leroy, 149
Post
  John, 86
  Saml., 43
Prenett
  Saml., 58

  Michael, 58
Ralston
Ramsey
  Eli, 134
  Ely, 134
  James, 5, 24, 42, 46, 59, 83, 84,

Saml., 64
Samuel, 62
Pricket Thos., 159 Jacob, 86
Prickett
  George, 73 Joseph, 55, 99, 115
Pruitt Jacob, 17, 20, 23, 24, 29
Pulliam Michal, 80 Wm., 16
Purcel
  Ignatius, 142, 147
Purcell
  John, 43
Purdue
  Larking, 10
Putman
  Jesse, 16, 20, 22, 24, 29, 31, 81, 101, 113
Putnam
  Jesse, 118
Quigly Wm., 101 Charles, 6
Quillian James, 36 Clemond, 104
Rabun
  William, 134, 152
  Wm., 136
Raburn
  William, 157
Ragsdale
  Wm., 106, 112, 117
Richardson
  Barbara, 29
  Riley
  Edward, 64
  James, 16, 31
  John, 100, 119
Robbin
  Wm., 27
Robert
  Aaron, 74
Roberts
  Woodson, 49, 50, 101
Robertson
  Jane, 24
  William, 24
  Wm., 24
Robins
  Mary, 27
  William, 31, 154
  Wm., 27, 34, 35, 41
Roe, 20, 95
  Richard, 6, 21, 49, 80, 88, 94, 111
  Richd., 7
Rogers
  Benjamin, 31

92, 95
Robert, 95
Wm., 25
Ratchford
  Patsey, 73 Redwine
Phillip, 5 Lewis, 159
Wm., 120
Reed
  David, 25
  James, 78, 87
  James, Jr., 74
  James, Sr., 101
  John, 147, 151, 156, 157
  Jos., 48, 49, 50, 52, 56, 92
  Joseph, 43, 46, 47, 56, 74, 78, 84, 92, 100, 119, 125, 129, 132, 133, 137
Reich
Reid
Reissun
  Price, 100
Reynolds
  Nancy, 64, 69, 113
Rice
  Charles, 16, 19, 22, 26, 27, 30
Rich
  Benjamin W., 18
Rose
  Drury, 39, 142, 144, 147, 149, 151, 155
Rucker
  George, Sr., 32
  John, 107
  John, Jr., 85
Runnels
  Bartimus, 14 Russell
  Stephen, 127
  William, 66
Ryly
  Edward, 94
  Edwd., 159
Sammond
  John, 90 Samson
  Wm., 43
Sanders
  Aaron, 142, 144, 147, 151, 155
  John, Jr., 42
  John, Sr., 16
  Moses, 16, 19, 27, 63, 69, 71
  Moses, Jr., 4, 9, 58
Sandidge
  Garrett L., 58, 144, 148, 155
Sandigde

G. L., 141
Sandige
  G. L., 62
  Garrett L., 75, 123
  John, 158
Sandridge
  G. L., 61
  Garrett L., 73
Sandrige
  G. L., 66
  Garrett L., 72, 106, 120
Sandwick
  Garrett L., 100
Sansom
  William, 22
Sartin
  Josiah, 142, 147
Satter
  Simon, 123
Savage
  Thos., 16, 100
Saxon
  Manoah, 5
  Robert, 4, 9, 10
  Robt., 74
Say
  Richard, 58, 62, 105, 113, 123
  Richd., 66, 72, 75, 100, 120
Scott
  Joseph J., 154
  Patrick, 120
  William, 37, 122
  Wm., 69, 106, 117, 147, 151
Seales
  Willis, 85
Seals
  Isaac C., 17
Selman
  John, 42
Sesser
  Charles, 74
Sessons
  Charles, 120
Sewel
  Jas., 101
  Wm., Sr., 146
Sewell
  Green, 32, 125, 127
  Green Berry, 34
  Green, Jr., 120
  Greenberry, 80, 126, 127, 128, 129, 130, 131, 133, 135, 136, 138
  James, 31, 34, 41
  Jno., 142
  John, 31, 34, 35, 85
  Moses, 142
  Nicholas, 74
Shankley
  Eli, 100
Shannan
  Saml., 100
Shannon
  Moses, 107
  Saml., 13, 16, 42, 148, 153
  Samuel, 4, 128, 144, 155
  Samul, 141
Sherell
  Georgia, 43
Sherill
  George, 22 Shockley
  Aquilla, 48
  Aquillia, 149

Richd., 142
Shotwell
  Reuben, 16, 19, 22, 27, 30, 74,
    78, 84, 100, 106, 113, 120, 123
Shuffield
  Adam, 46, 47, 52, 55, 61, 66
  Averet, 125
Simmons
  John, 122, 123
Simms
  Phil. L., 38
Sims
  Martin, 31
Sisson
  Charles, 100, 105, 118, 123, 156, 157
Sissons
  Charles, 17
Skelton
  Robert, 90, 100
Slater
  Benjn., 74
Slocum
  Christopher M., 14
  William, 14
Smith
  Allen, 146
  Edward D., 91
  Gabriel, 5, 74
  Green W., 41, 60, 61, 76, 82, 105, 127, 131
  Henrey, 155
  Henry, 4, 15, 70, 74, 78, 84, 141, 144, 148
  Hez., 86
  Hezekiah, 89, 147, 151

J., 33, 57, 66
James, 26, 28, 71, 83, 130, 140
Jas., 85
Jesse, 31, 119, 159
John, 43, 47, 70
John M., 147, 148, 151, 152, 153
Miles, 107
Nathan, 20, 109
Noah, 146, 154
Peter, 64
Richard, 26, 106, 115, 150
Richd., 109
Robert, 125
Thos., 101, 106, 112, 117, 151
Victor, 122, 159
William, 129, 134, 140
Wm., 58, 100, 103, 106, 112, 117
Wmson., 134
Spark
  Elijah, 127
Sparks
  Elijah, 36, 47, 108, 120, 121
  Jeremiah, 32, 92
  Jerh., 101
  Thos., Sr., 5
Spears
  William, 20
Starrett
  Benj., 46
  Benjamin, 56, 76, 77
  Benjn., 158
  James, 42, 47, 107
Starritt
  B., 45
  Benj., 42
  Benjamin, 45
Statham

Nathl., 5
Stephens
  Hezekiah, 63, 69, 71
  Hezk., 58
Stevenson
  Becca, 50
Stiles
  William, 26, 106, 115, 149
Stonecypher
  James, 159
  John, 31, 34, 35, 36, 41
Story
  Anthoney, 84, 105, 119, 125, 129, 132, 137
  Anthony, 74, 78, 100, 133
  Thomas., 101
Stovall
  George, 15, 34, 35, 41, 85, 89, 96, 99, 102, 119, 121, 125, 129, 132, 133, 137, 139
  George, Jr., 31
  Georgia, 4
  Jos., 17, 18
  Josiah, 5, 14, 42, 46
Stow
  Warren, 101, 126, 132
Stoydon
  Benjamin, 9
Strang
  Starling, 86
Strange
  Edmund, 31
  Joel, 58
  Seth, 85, 89, 96, 99, 102, 141
  Starling, 4, 68, 92
  Stephen, 9
  Sterling, 10, 71

Strickland, 22
  Aron, 46
  Isaac, 8, 10, 11, 22, 90, 103
  Wilson, 10, 11
Stubbs
  John, 31, 34, 35, 41
Studley
  William, 111
Studly
  William, 88
Sutton
  John, 76, 107
Swan
  Edward, Sr., 150
Swann
  Edward, Jr., 146, 150
  Edward, Sr., 146, 150 Edwd., 150
Swife
  Tyre, 91
Swift
  John, 14
  Tyre, 17
Swit
  Tyre, 86
Tabar
  Zach, 43
Tabor
  Adkins, 108
  Adkinson, 149
  Atkins, 17, 101
  John, 48, 49, 50
  Jos., 49
Tait
  James, 78, 100, 118, 123, 155
  Jas., 35
  Saml., 5

Talbert
  Alexander, 39
Tarsey
  William, 20 Tate
  Andrew, 48
  James, 40, 74, 84, 105, 118, 141, 144, 148, 150, 151, 153, 158
  John, 76, 87
  Samuel, 27, 50, 52
  William, 63
Tayler
  Jeremiah, 146
  Wm., 142
Taylor
  Ann, 73
  Arthur, 120
  Charles, 73
  Elizabeth, 73
  Geo., 86
  Geo. C., 73
  George, 20, 22, 24
  George ___, 17
  George C., 5, 73
  Georgia, 29
  Hugh, 14
  Jeremiah, 142, 147, 151, 155
  Jeremiah, Jr., 55
  Joseph, 110, 114
  Levi T., 101
  Patsey, 73
  Robert, 127
Temples
  Jno., 85
  John, 17, 20, 23, 24, 29, 35, 89, 154
Terrel
  John D., 13
Terrell, 13, 130
  H., 26
  Hezekiah, 24, 26, 27, 160
  Jno. D., 144
  John D., 14, 17, 42, 47, 90, 103
  Joseph, 31, 34, 35, 41, 74, 78
  Peter B., 27
  Simon, 20, 31, 74, 109, 119
  Timothy, 17, 58, 76, 85, 89, 99, 102, 141, 144, 146 Wm., 32
Thomas, 93
  Jesse, 107, 125, 132
  Joel, 159
  William, 24
  Wm., 74, 78, 84, 119
Thompson
  Darby, 25
  Farley, 27, 39, 45, 96
  William, 33
Thornton
  David, 43, 142
  Elijah, 119, 125, 127, 129, 135, 138
  Reuben, 119, 125, 127, 129, 135, 138
Thrasher
  Benedict, 111
  Benja.,   88
  Salley, 88
  Sally, 111
Thurmond
  Fountain, 122
Tilman
  Aaron, 43
  George, 59

Tindal
  Parnal, 111
  Purnal, 133, 152
  Salah, 152
  Sally, 111
Tindall
  Sally, 133, 152
Tolbert
  Patience, 112, 138
  Washington, 112, 138
Tollison
  Eli, 101
Toney
  Charles, 106, 107, 112, 117
  Chas., 101
  Harris, 123
Townsend
  John, 101
  Thomas, 145
  Thomas, Jr., 55
Towsen
  Thos., 119
Tracey
  Charles, 31
Tranham
  Absalom, 119 Trantham
  Absalam, 125
  Absalom, 70, 127, 129, 135
Trigg
  John, 84, 92, 95, 109, 110, 114, 116, 127, 141, 143, 147, 148, 160
Trimble
  John, 42, 46
  Moses, 142, 147
Troman
  George, 50
Troy
  John, 43
Tucker
  Benjamin, 134, 138, 142, 143
  Benjn., 58, 92, 126
  William, 32, 78, 90
  Wm., 74
Turk
  Margaret, 51, 99
  Wm., 99, 108
Turman
  Geo., 69
  George, 64, 69, 70, 108, 113
Upson
  S., 86
  Stephen, 159, 160
Vannum
  Jno., 142
Vaughan
  George, 131
  John, 12
Verdel
  John A., 35
Vessell
  Ephram, 159
  James, 159
Vines
  Benjamin, 106
Wade
  Nathaniel, 71
Waggoner
  Peter, 68
Wagner
  Peter, 25
Wagnon
  Peter, 72

Walraven
  William, 27
Walter
  Joseph, 78
Walters
  Clemt., 42
  Elijah, 43
  Jos., 84
  Joseph, 30, 74, 125
  Moses, 31
  Robert, 4, 13, 144, 150, 151, 155
  Robert, Jr., 17, 146
  Robt., 146
  Robt., Jr., 142
Walton
  Jesse, 115
  Killis, 17
  Newal, Sr., 48
  Newell, 106, 115, 150
Wammack
  John, 155
Ward
  Ann, 142
  Bryan, 36, 66
  Charles, 121, 153
  James, 36 John, 142
  Joshua, 119
  Saml., 36
  Samuel, 37, 153
  William, 96, 144
  Wm., 34, 35, 41, 74, 85, 89, 99, 102, 141, 146
Wardon
  Roland, 159
Warmack
  John, 30, 100, 142, 144

Warmock
  Jno., 27
Warren
  Charles, 21, 52
  Reuben, 32
Waters
  Robert, 16
Watkins
  George, 59
  Robert, 107
  Robert H., 139
Watson
  James C., 118
Watters
  John C., 59
  Joseph, 16, 19, 27, 70
  Peter, 98
  Robert, 8, 147
Weems
  Redfearn, 62, 75, 106, 118
  Redfern, 16, 58, 72, 100, 123
West
  John, 11, 13
Westbrook
  John, 75, 103, 132
  Stephen, 28, 42, 75, 148, 149
  Wm., 74, 78
Westbrooks
  John, 6
  Stephen, 22, 30, 103
  Wm., 87
Whipple
  Jesse, 131, 140
Whisenhunt
  Adam, 16, 19, 22, 30
  Jacob, 7

Whitaker
  Benjamin, 152, 156, 157
White
  Jacob, Jr., 119
  Jeptha, 119
  Joseph, 17
  Rachel, 107
  Richard, 139
  Samuel, 159
  Thomas, 72, 83
  Thos., 5
  Zachariah, 83
Whitehead
  Benja., 17, 40
  Burrell, 142, 144, 147, 151, 155
  Jos., 86
Whitney, 68
  Wm. O., 68
Whordlow
  James, 106
Wilhite
  M. T., 139
Wilkenson
  Jas., 142
Wilkerson
  Willm., 32 Wm., 142
Wilkins
  Thomas, 45, 103, 140
  Thos., 103, 154
Wilkinson
  Elisha, 13, 57, 60
  James, 8
  Wm. H., 144, 147
Wilkison
  James, 5
Williams
  ___, 142
  Deloney, 122, 137
  Francis, 48, 87, 89, 94
  Jas., 159
  John, 40, 86, 91
  Lewis, 48
  Louis, 17
  Martin, 70
  Nancy, 122, 137
  Nathaniel, 147
  Nathl., 58, 69, 71, 144, 151, 155
  Patsy, 154
  Robert, 58, 159
  Robt., 142
Williamson
  Alexander, 7, 37, 122
  Geo., 86
  James, 5, 8, 9, 10, 26, 63, 69
  Jas., 59
  John, 26
  P., 44
  Peter, 44, 51, 60
  Robert, 129, 132
  Samuel, 26
  Sarah, 26 Wm., 26
Willis, 126, 158
Wilson
  Benjamin, 112
  William, 17
  Wm., 58, 62, 64
Wims
  Redfearn, 19, 22, 27, 30, 118
Winn
  Hamilton, 158
Wise
  Joseph, 24

Wofford
  Benjamin, 78
  Benjn., 74
  James, 58
  Nathaniel, 52, 127, 158
  Nathanl., 17, 58
  Nathl., 62, 66, 72, 100, 119
  William, 130
  William B., 44, 51, 118, 122
  William H., 154
  Wm., 43
  Wm. B., 53
Womack
  John, 16, 141
Wood, 65
  Elias, 69, 70, 72
  Richd., 16, 42, 79
  Richd., Jr., 43
  William, 31, 83
Woodall
  Charity, 7, 37 Joseph, 8, 56
Woods
  Nancy, 128
  Richard, 30, 128
Word
Yawel

  Joel, 124

Yeargan

  Samuel, 158

Yowel

  Charles, 47
  Wm., 96
Worel
  Charles, 36
Wormack
  John, 19, 22, 74
Wright
  Jno., 86
  John, 90
Wryly
  John, 58
Wyley
  James R., 41
Wyly
  James R., 31, 34, 66
Yarborough Grove, 10
  Groves, 9, 147
Yarbour
  Groves, 142
Yarbrough
  Groves, 4, 144
  Jeptha, 99
Yates
  Joseph, 15, 151, 153

  Joel, 47, 112, 150

  Joshua, 148

Yowell

  Joel, 31, 34, 36, 41, 115

  Joshua, 109, 121, 124

www.ingramcontent.com/pod-product-compliance
Lightning Source LLC
Chambersburg PA
CBHW020650300426
44112CB00007B/321